BUILDING CHILDREN'S MINISTRY

A Practical Guide

TINA HOUSER

Published by
THOMAS NELSON™
Since 1798

www.thomasnelson.com

Published in Nashville, Tennessee, by Thomas Nelson. Thomas Nelson is a trademark of Thomas Nelson, Inc.

Thomas Nelson, Inc., titles may be purchased in bulk for educational, business, fund-raising, or sales promotional use. For information, please e-mail SpecialMarkets@ThomasNelson.com.

Unless otherwise noted, Scripture quotations are taken from the *Holy Bible*, New Living Translation. © 1996. Used by permission of Tyndale House Publishers, Inc., Wheaton, Illinois 60189. All rights reserved.

Scripture quotations marked NIV are taken from the HOLY BIBLE: NEW INTERNATIONAL VERSION®. © 1973, 1978, 1984 by International Bible Society. Used by permission of Zondervan Publishing House. All rights reserved.

Scripture quotations marked MSG are taken from *The Message* by Eugene H. Peterson, © 1993, 1994, 1995, 1996, 2000. Used by permission of Nav Press Publishing Group. All rights reserved.

Library of Congress Cataloging-in-Publication Data

Houser, Tina.
 Building children's ministry : a practical guide / Tina Houser.
   p. cm.
 Includes index.
 ISBN-13: 978-1-4185-2681-8
 ISBN-10: 1-4185-2681-9
 1. Church work with children. I. Title.
BV639.C4H68 2007
259'.22--dc22

                          2007047179

Printed in the United States of America
1 2 3 4 5 6 —12 11 10 09 08

TABLE OF CONTENTS

ACKNOWLEDGMENTS

I feel like the cell phone commercial that shows the customer accompanied by a mass of people. Wherever the customer goes, the support staff of the company goes, although unnoticed most of the time. As I look back at how I got to this point in children's ministry and how this book came about, I see a mass of people cheering me on and helping me make good connections. They all deserve more thanks than I can give them.

First of all, I want to thank all the parents and children who have welcomed me into their lives, and who have trusted that even my craziest moments have a point to them. Each one has taught me something valuable that makes me better at what God has given me to do. I love being a children's pastor! The joy God gives me through these kids is absolutely indescribable.

Thank you to my husband, Ray, for making his first words every morning, "I love you," and to my son, Jarad, who thinks more highly of me than I could ever deserve.

Thank you to the many people who participate in the children's ministry team at First Church of God in Kokomo, Indiana. They inspire me to stretch my leadership skills and expand the boundaries of my creativity. They make me look good!

And, thank you to an old friend whom I've known since my early elementary years, Neil Brewer, who allowed me to use a poem he wrote about school days.

Thank you to Michael Stephens, my editor, who embraced the vision and saw the importance of writing a book on starting children's ministry. I have had many questions as we've gone through this process, and he has patiently answered each one.

And to all the people at my workshops who have persistently asked for a book of this kind, thank you for encouraging me to keep writing. Here it is! It has been doused with prayer, laughter, tears, and goose bumps. May you turn the eyes of children toward the One who created and adores them.

1

PREPARING THE SITE

Let me roll out the red carpet and welcome you to the world of children's ministry. Since you've picked up this book, children must be im--portant to you. That means you and I are on the same page and I am thrilled to be working arm-in-arm with you.

The set of blueprints that are laid before you in the Table of Contents are not for a dream house or a new shopping center or any other building made of bricks and mortar. Instead, these blueprints are for building people—people who will be a big part of your life for years to come, as well as people you will never even meet. This is where the dreams you have for children's ministry can begin to take form, and then prosper. God has a plan for you as well as the children's ministry you are part of, and it's a good plan. Jeremiah 29:11 assures us that God has a plan for each of us—a good plan, not for disaster—a plan that opens up the future and gives us hope. When that verse runs through my head and I think about it in terms of children's ministry, I can feel my heart begin to pound and my blood start to run faster through my veins.

When I was in third grade, my parents decided to build a home in a new subdivision. The huge roll of blueprints that the builders kept looking at made no sense to me. What I wanted was to have my very own bedroom, to have beautiful new furniture, and a recreation room where my friends could come over to hang out. What I envisioned was the end result. Fortunately, there were key people who paid great attention to the little lines and markings on those blueprints so that my end result wishes could happen.

What I want to do in the pages of this book is help you think through the blueprints of children's ministry. What steps should we take to assure that we are offering a comprehensive scriptural foundation for children? Coming up with programs before the foundation is laid, if you will pardon the old adage, is like "putting the cart before the horse." For instance, someone wants to start a puppet team and calls it children's ministry. Another person works with a group of children to memorize Scripture and calls it children's ministry. But no one has stopped to make a plan, to draw up the blueprints. Consequently, what happens is that the different programs are happening without a connection or understandable objective. These programs are good things to do, but their purpose in the body of Christ is not understood.

Every night my entire family drove out to the site of our new house to check on that day's progress. Sometimes weeks passed and I didn't notice any changes. At other times, the change in one day would be remarkable, like the day the landscaping was put in. Our new house took on a completely different look. That's how it's going to be with creating a children's ministry. The Table of Contents shows you what's involved in laying the foundation. It involves things like understanding the purpose of the ministry, setting objectives, raising up trained workers, designing a security plan, and creating a budget. All these things take place mostly behind the scenes. It will seem as though there's no progress for long periods of time, but when the foundation is laid correctly, the finished work—the exciting and attractive programs—will have a definite role to play in the entire plan. Can you work for a while behind the scenes laying the foundation? If you invest the time now, I can assure you that the children's ministry you are creating will have fewer loose ends, a sense of purpose, and less conflict. (And don't we all want that!) That's the outcome when the boundaries are set and the foundation is laid, so let's look at putting things in the right order. A house that does not have a good foundation will not stand the test of time.

Every day I spend time talking with children's pastors who are new to this field of ministry. Many of their questions are the same. We chat via e-mail or over the phone and discuss this incredible calling that God has given us. In an attempt to be more effective personally, this book is my way of sitting down to chat about some of the issues that those of you who are new to children's ministry will face. Be encouraged! It's been a wonderful venture for me and I know it can be the same for you.

WHY CHILDREN'S MINISTRY IS IMPORTANT

It's time to step out of the shadows of what children's ministry has been in the past. We're no longer just talking about childcare; we're talking about touching the hearts and minds of children so that they will desire to live godly lives. Children's ministry is about building followers of Christ from physical infancy, rather than waiting until children become adults and having to tear down the building and rebuild. Why is it important? Because God says so, that's why!

It Is Close to God's Heart

Children's ministry is important because it's close to the heart of God. Get a concordance and look up the references to children. There are so many! Some of the verses are simply listing "women and children" involved in an event, but most are referring to God's people. These are not necessarily references to the young age of people, but rather show that children are so highly regarded that God even refers to adults who possess childlike qualities as children. In Matthew 18:3, God elevates children by saying "unless you turn from your sins and become like little children, you will never get into the Kingdom of Heaven." The scripture is telling us that we should aspire to be like children, because the traits they possess are what God is looking for in His people. Believers are lovingly called children in 1 John 5:1: "Everyone who believes that Jesus is the Christ has become a child of God. And everyone who loves the Father loves his children, too." Yes indeed, children are close to the heart of God!

God Commanded It

God has commanded us to reach children. Deuteronomy 32:46 says, "Pass them on as a command to your children so they will obey every word of these instructions." And, Deuteronomy 11:19 tells us, "Teach them to your children. Talk about them when you are at home and when you are on the road, when you are going to bed and when you are getting up." We have our orders. This is the core of how we do children's ministry. It happens anywhere, at any time, using anything to get the point across. There is a plea for everyone to help raise up a godly generation. We must *just do it* because God tells us to.

We Learn from the Past

Children's ministry is one huge way that we pass on the faith to others. God told Joshua to build a stone memorial at the campsite next to the Jordan River, so that when the next generation saw the memorial they would ask what it stood for. (God was setting up an object lesson for future generations!) Then, the children could be told how the Israelites crossed the Jordan and how the walls of Jericho fell to God's glory (Josh. 4). What happened in the faith journey of generations past is important to the children of this generation. We learn from and are inspired by the successes and failures of our faithful ancestors. Children must be told.

It's a Source of Joy

Getting kids to connect on a spiritual level is important and a source of joy. Proverbs 23:24 tells us, "The father of godly children has cause for joy. What a pleasure to have children who are wise." God wants to give us joy, and one way He does that is through raising up godly children. They bless Him, and they bless us.

Our Brains Are Designed that Way

Here's a reason that's going to raise your eyebrows. Children's ministry is important because of the way God designed our brains. As I write this, I am so excited about this discovery that I'm bouncing up and down in my chair. I just hope I can help you see the impact of having this information. While taking a college course a few years ago I made an amazing discovery. The professor showed three pictures of the neuropaths in the same brain at different stages of childhood. The first picture was taken when the child was about six months old. The lines depicting the neuropaths were trailing around the brain, indicating that the infant was beginning to take in information. The second picture was taken at six years old. The brain was a matted mess with neuropaths crisscrossing one another, evidence of the child taking in and holding onto a huge amount of information. This didn't surprise me in the least, as I've witnessed how preschoolers are sponges. The third picture was the one that took me by surprise. It had been taken around the age of fourteen. Many of the lines had disappeared. Where did they go? Where was that mass of information? I was expecting a picture that was completely solid with pathways. Instead, I saw a much less complicated picture. The professor explained that around the age of twelve, the brain begins a very interesting process. It starts doing an inventory and review of the information stored there, keeping what is being used regularly, and filing away information that isn't being used consistently. God made us that way! Incredible! Interesting, but what does that have to do with children's ministry? It has everything to do with children's ministry. Research done by the Barna Group and compiled in *Transforming Children into Spiritual Champions* indicates that personal moral foundations regarding values, morality, and truth are in place by the age of thirteen and are incredibly difficult to change after that. Understanding the physical development of the brain explains the Barna research results.

Not only do children need to be taught the Bible, they need to be using it regularly for their brains to acknowledge its necessity and not physically discard it. When I looked at different areas of the Christian life, such as service, prayer, and personal time of devotion, I realized that we couldn't just teach about them, we had to make them real for kids. We had to intentionally teach these disciplines. If kids weren't actually being given opportunities to serve, to be engaged in meaningful prayer time, to participate in tithing, and to consistently take time for personal devotions, then around their twelfth birthday, their brains would feel that those aspects of the Christian life weren't worth keeping around. We've got to get desperate about reaching kids. The clock is ticking! Each day they get closer to age twelve and to the time when their brains will begin to discard what's not being used.

We've got to take this seriously because evil influences take it seriously. The world already understands how impressionable and formidable these young years are. The Barna research indicates that the values that become the heart and soul of a child before the teen years are the values most likely kept throughout adulthood. It goes both ways. Those can be godly values or they can be worldly values. It doesn't take a rocket scientist to look around and find evidence of evil at work in our children's lives. Is there evidence as easily found for God's people at work for the sake of children?

I am so thankful that George Barna took the time and yielded to God's prompting to gather these facts and do this research. Read *Transforming Children into Spiritual Champions* or visit www.barna.org and you'll agree with Barna's conclusion: the church needs to make children's ministry its number one priority!

Ministry to children is a high and holy calling. Because of the faithful ones who refuse to let anything get in the way of bringing children into a relationship with a God who loves them personally, this new generation will hear God's message and make godly decisions. "Our children will also serve him. Future generations will hear about the wonders of the Lord" (Ps. 22:30). What an honor. What a privilege. How humbling it is to be called to pass God's Word on to children.

CREATE A STATEMENT OF PURPOSE

One of the most critical elements of beginning a children's ministry is establishing a statement of purpose. If you are years into children's ministry and don't have a statement of purpose, stop right now and put one together. Your statement of purpose is your blueprint. This is what you gauge all your programs by. It can guide you to move forward with a new venture or it can reveal that you're going in the wrong direction. Some people call this a statement of purpose, others call it a mission statement, overall objectives, a visioning statement, or a philosophy. Some churches think they need to have a mission statement, as well as a visioning statement, and a philosophy. Essentially, what they have done is gotten more specific with each level as they break it down. Whatever term you want to give this statement, you need to have something written down that is going to tell you what your children's ministry is about. Who is it supposed to reach? What types of activities happen within it? And, what are the boundaries that keep it focused as a ministry of your church? What sets it apart from other things happening in your community?

We will talk repeatedly about the fact that children's ministry should be integrated into the church body. The children's ministry statement of purpose should parallel the purpose of the church. If the purpose of the church reflects missions as a high priority, then the children's ministry needs to develop specific programming that will educate children about missions and give them the opportunity to participate. If the church mission statement is weighted toward tackling needs specific to the inner city, then the children's ministry should keep those same needs in mind in everything it does. The church's statement of purpose should not go in one direction while the children's ministry's statement of purpose goes in another. Let me show you how our church's statement of purpose and our children's ministry's statement align.

The purpose of First Church of God, Kokomo, Indiana, is to glorify God by:

❁ Reaching out to those who don't know Christ with the message of salvation and discipleship.

❁ Growing up to be like Jesus in our thinking, standards, and maturity.

❁ Growing together in the fellowship of Christian love for each other.

❁ Lifting up those in need in our community and world simply because they are in need and we have help to offer.

A well-written purpose statement will be concise and easy to understand. It should be written so people can get it in their heads and in their hearts. It is evident that our church's statement of purpose speaks with passion about what we want to accomplish and it can easily be simplified into: Reach Out, Grow Up, Grow Together, and Lift Up . . . and do it

REACH OUT

...to the kids in our community
- TNT
- POP
- 2 VBSs
- Christmas Craft Day

...to encourage a commitment to Christ
- Jr. Church
- Baptism Class
- GodCalling@YourHeart.com
- Summer Camp

GROW UP

Provide Time of Worship
- Jr. Church
- Little Flock
- Joyful Noise
- David's Parade
- GodCalling@YourHeart.com

Teach Bible Knowledge
- Sunday School
- TNT
- POP
- Jr. Church
- Little Flock
- VBS

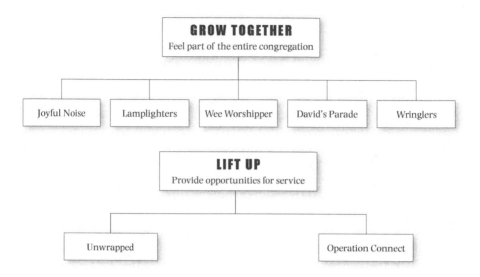

all to glorify God. There was no need for us to have a different, reworded statement of purpose. These four points give direction to the church and establish its personality. If the children are truly a vital part of the congregation, then the children's ministry leadership has the huge task of making sure that all four of these purposes are integrated into the children's ministry programming. If the church's statement of purpose feels vague to you, then list what it means to children's ministry under each point, clarifying what kind of actions it requires.

We took each of our four statements and put them on a card on the wall. We then took a close look at each of our children's ministry programs to see what their specific objectives were. Work diligently at understanding that all programs do not have to fulfill all objectives, but all objectives do need to be met through some means. On another card we wrote the name of the program and taped it underneath as many headings as it applied to. This gave us a visual instrument to use in interpreting the weight each of the four points in our statement were getting in the children's ministry. It also helped us identify areas that were weak or nonexistent.

One of the great benefits of keeping the statement of purpose and its breakdown in front of you at all times is the process of evaluation it puts in place when someone comes to you and wants to do a certain event or thinks a program should be started. You raise a few questions based on the statement of purpose when making this decision: What are the objectives of this new program? Do those objectives fit firmly into our statement of purpose? Is this event or program filling a hole in our ministry or is it adding more to one area of an already overloaded programming schedule. Occasionally, an overzealous person will come to you convinced that the church should carry out a special event. It sounds like a lot of fun, but that's all it is—fun! Okay, so we need to be able to enjoy one another, "growing together in the fellowship of Christian love for each other." But, as we look closely at the successful programs that are in place, we notice that our times of fellowship are far surpassing the other areas of purpose. Our goal is to keep all areas of our statement of purpose in balance. If our fellowship time is already loaded with activity, then our energies should be placed somewhere else, and you can suggest that a club or school might want to plan this particular event.

On the other hand, evaluating the weight of your programs in this way can also point out your inadequacies. That's what we found. Under the heading of "reaching out to those who don't know Christ with the message of salvation and discipleship" (which we basically think of as outreach and evangelism), we placed our midweek evening programs, TNT and POP. Also, under that heading fell both of our VBS weeks, which include outreach as the prime objective, and our special events, such as Christmas Craft Day where we invite children throughout our community to bring their parents for several hours of making Christmas crafts. Junior Church and our summer camping programs are also highly evangelistic. We patted ourselves on the back because we felt like we were taking advantage of opportunities to reach out to our community and speak the Word of God. We were fulfilling this purpose well.

When we looked at how we program for "growing up to be like Jesus in our thinking, standards, and maturity" we thought about activities that provided a time to worship and absorb Bible knowledge. We identified our older Junior Church and our younger Junior Church (called Little Flock), our thriving Sunday school, the midweek programs previously mentioned (TNT and POP), both VBS programs, and Godcalling@yourheart.com, which is an intensive discipleship program helping children consider God's plan for their life. So, we thought we were doing admirably in the "growing up" area.

As we evaluated "growing together in the fellowship of Christian love for each other" it was easy to see that our children feel invested in worship services where the entire church body comes together and we were indeed growing together as a church family. Joyful Noise is our elementary-age children's choir that participates every third week in morning worship and brings a sparkle to the service. Wee Worshippers, which is a musical experience for three- and four-year-olds, enjoy their special times when they contribute to corporate worship. In addition, David's Parade (a sign language/interpretive movement program during the summer), Wringlers (a handbell choir for preschoolers during the summer), and Lamplighters (where kids memorize large portions of Scripture) all make significant contributions to worship times. Bravo! We were three for three!

And, lastly, we looked at how we were "lifting up those in need in our community and world simply because they are in need and we have help to offer." We scoured through the programs and then stopped dead in our tracks. We had been on such a roll and we were almost finished. Yes, we taught about missions once in a while in Sunday school and Junior Church, but it wasn't a primary objective. We did a service project at Christmas, and the children made cards occasionally to send to our soldiers. But, were we intentionally teaching children to serve their community and the world? After taking a hard look at everything, we had to admit that children's ministry was falling short in this area. So, before we added anything to any other area, we decided to "fill" this hole in our ministry. A long search through curricula and questioning children's pastors all over the country told us that we weren't alone. So, we designed a program called "Unwrapped" where second and third graders spend six weeks learning about and experiencing serving others in their homes, their churches, their communities, and the world. It was extremely experiential and life-changing. The adults sat up and took notice of how the children were putting feet and hands to the concept of serving. They watched the foundational mind-set of servanthood take hold. This idea of intentionally serving caught on with the entire church. Imagine how the children felt when adults were stealing their ideas and small groups were putting into action what the children had begun. It was a tremendous boost to the children, who realized they were able to lead adults. The message came through loud and clear that they truly are an essential part of the church body. Without our evaluation tool—our statement of purpose—we would not have recognized where we needed help.

Some of you are asking what to do if the leadership in your church has not felt the need to create a statement of purpose for the entire church. First of all, gently and convincingly show those in authority that this really needs to be done for the church so that everyone—staff and laypeople alike—has the same goals and expectations. And, once established, it needs to be kept in front of the people at all times: interspersed in PowerPoint announcements, in brochures, in the Sunday bulletin, on Web sites, and in any other published material. Getting the church to understand the need and then act on it, though, may be a

long process. Don't be afraid to take the lead! If you feel that you're stepping over your boundaries, then make your statement of purpose something less intrusive by calling it your guidelines, your goals, or your target. When I talk about goals with my kids, I frequently use an activity
where I set the kids loose to throw sponge balls at a big blank wall. Then,
I ask them how they did. Immediately, they respond that they didn't
know how they did, but they had fun doing it. They usually also decide
that they were getting tired of it real quick. Without a statement of purpose—a target, a goal, guidelines—we may have some fun programs,
but we don't really know if we accomplished what we were supposed to.
And, just as importantly, your workers wear down more quickly because
they don't know what is expected of them.

Let's return to the activity with my kids. In the second part of the
game I put down masking tape lines on the floor and place targets on
the wall. I tell the kids that they have to stand behind the line to throw
and they get a certain number of points for hitting different areas of the
target. This time when I ask them how they did, each child is able to give
a definite answer. There is an old saying, "If you aim at nothing, you are
sure to hit it." That rings true when we're contemplating a statement of
purpose for children's ministry.

It would be so easy to jump on the bandwagon of every new program that comes along and send yourself and your staff to the point of
exhaustion on the fast train. Some of those programs or curricula fit
your purpose statement while others don't. Add them if there is a need
and a place, but don't be afraid to pass them by if they don't fit into your
balance. This doesn't mean they're not great programs—there's another
church somewhere (maybe even down the street from you) that will see
the program as a perfect fit for what they are doing with children. Keeping an attentive eye on the balance of programs under your statement
of purpose will leave you with a well-rounded children's ministry that

you can be confident is giving children the opportunity to grow in all areas of their spirituality.

CAST THE VISION

"Vision is the art of seeing the invisible."
—Jonathan Swift

There is a Native American legend that speaks of a wise father who was nearing the end of his life. He had three sons and he wanted to leave everything he owned to the son who proved himself brave and full of promise. The father decided to send each of the three sons on a mission. With the three young men standing in front of him, he pointed to the mountain that towered in the distance. The sons were told to make a trip up the mountain and bring back something that showed how far they had traveled up the mountainside. The first son returned and placed a bouquet of beautiful white flowers in his father's hands. The father smiled for he knew the flowers grew just beyond the timberline and that the young man had traveled far. The second son returned and handed the old man some red flint stones. These stones were found very near to the top of the mountain and the father smiled. The old man waited patiently for the third son to return. It was a long time. Finally, the third son appeared before his father, empty-handed, but with a smile on his face. He excitedly explained to his father that where he went there was nothing to bring back. "I went to the summit, Father, and looked out across a gorgeous valley. I saw rivers I had never seen before, and a body of water that met the horizon. It was the most exciting thing I have ever experienced!" The wise old man nodded in agreement, for he knew what this son spoke of. He spoke to the boy, from the deepest part of his heart, of his desire that one of his sons would see what he had seen and experienced: "My dear son, you have nothing in your hands, but you have something far greater in your heart and spirit. You have a vision in your soul."

The third young son experienced something greater than he had ever imagined and witnessed, something he had never dreamed of. He looked beyond what he knew. The others were satisfied to appreciate what was within their grasp. The vision for your children's ministry, whether it is the overall vision or the specific vision you have for one dynamic program and the people attached to it, should always be bigger than you have imagined or dreamed about. That way, you will have to trust in God to make it happen. In Ephesians 3:20, the Scriptures tell us that, "Through his mighty power at work within us, he is able to accomplish infinitely more than we might ask or think."

Before we go any further, let's define *vision*. *Vision* is the picture we have in our mind's eye of the ideal future for specific individuals (such as children). It begins with the recognition of an incredible opportunity. The picture gets clearer in your mind and the conviction that this opportunity is important grows persistently in you. You come to a place where you believe without a doubt that this is something God has given and has ordained. You may wonder how in the world it's going to be accomplished, but you're convinced that it needs to happen. And there it lies—swirling around in your mind, causing butterflies in your stomach—creating excitement and momentum.

That's where the "casting" comes in. How do you get other people to come alongside you? How do you get them to embrace this vision and make it their own? How do you communicate effectively enough that they see the same picture you see? How do you get them excited? Have you ever seen the Sunday school papers where kids are asked to get the lame man through the maze and into the pool? You can see the man in a corner of the page. You can see the pool in another corner. But, how do you get through the maze? It's the same with having a vision and getting others to believe in it. You know what the vision is and you can see it accomplished in one corner. You know who needs to come onboard and connect with the vision. But how do you take those people on the journey from brainstorming to implementation?

Because you're reading this book, I'm assuming that God has been revealing His plan to you, a plan that includes ministering to children. I came into children's ministry twenty-eight years ago at a time when my husband was a youth pastor in Fresno, California. His job description changed unexpectedly to include a ministry to children. Our Sunday afternoons were miserable, because he spent most of it complaining about how uncomfortable and misplaced he felt working with kids. Finally, in order to bring some sanity back into our Sunday afternoons, I gave him the opportunity to bow out and I stepped in. That was the "divine" motivation for beginning my ministry with kids. It took years for me to see God's vision for children's ministry. It wasn't something I woke up thinking about in the morning. The endearing comment of a child did not delight my spirit for an entire day. I had no dream for what could happen if I poured myself into this. God, on the other hand, was at work, diligently planting the seeds that would grow into a passion that I could not put down and a vision that I didn't want to take my eyes off. Don't be so anxious that you impatiently try to rush God's work. He has a plan for children's ministry where you are, and I'm sure it includes you. Let Him give you that picture of what He wants to accomplish in you and through you. Then, hold on tight, because you're in for a better ride than any roller coaster can offer!

The ability to cast a vision in the workplace, where those who fall under your leadership are obligated by their job security to buy into the vision, is both similar to and different from casting a vision with volunteers. The main difference is that they don't have to follow. Some people even say that the true test of leadership is to put people in volunteer positions and see if they will follow voluntarily. True leaders will surface with a crowd of devoted and willing supporters who have bought into the vision they see for the organization. It would be difficult to say that vision casting is the most important tool you need in building a strong children's ministry, just as it would be difficult to say the hammer is the most important tool in building a home, because each tool is reliant on the successful use of the others. But, we *can* say that being able to successfully cast a vision for your ministry is definitely an indispensable tool.

Leaders who fail to see the importance of casting a vision are setting themselves up for a lonely failure. Telling people what to do without creating the picture of what is going to happen because of their efforts is like shooting fireworks into the air, creating a fleeting ooh-ahh moment, only to have it quickly fizzle out. Without a vivid vision present in the hearts and minds of your team, it will be extremely difficult to keep them in that ooh-ahh state of mind and from moving into the fizzled-out stage.

The Bible is full of instances of vision casting. Joseph was able to convince the pharaoh and all of Egypt that they needed to prepare for a famine that would occur in seven years (Gen. 41:25–57). The people willingly followed Joseph, because he was able to communicate the urgency of the task and how his plan would meet a desperate need. Josiah delivered the vision of the temple restored and of Scripture being respected and obeyed. Even though he was a young king, when the people witnessed his excitement over the discovery of the holy scrolls, they willingly followed and joined him (2 Kings 22:1–23:25). When Philip asked the Ethiopian if he understood the scripture he was reading, the Ethiopian replied, "How can I if no one helps me?" Philip cast the vision of salvation to the Ethiopian and the man responded by believing in Jesus Christ as his Savior. The Ethiopian embraced the vision and the Bible tells us that he was eager to tell the people of his country about Jesus (Acts 8:26–39).

In the three stories just mentioned, there is some amazing vision casting taking place, and it happened because of effective communication. These stories have given us important considerations for how we are to be vision casters in children's ministry.

Joseph had a plan and he communicated his plan well. His plan included how the people would have to save their supplies for the first seven years and it also took into consideration how those supplies would be distributed during the second seven years. Casting a vision has a lot to do with getting people to see the end result, but it also involves the nuts and bolts of how to get there. Some people have difficulty wrapping their arms and their hearts around a vision that is bigger than they understand, but they can embrace the smaller ideas that move toward the big vision. When I began as Minister of Children at First Church of God in Kokomo, Indiana, about fifteen years ago, I envisioned a church where children were present in every part of the ministry of the church and a church that was known throughout the community for the way it touched the lives of children. Now, we have sixteen programs that kids can be involved in throughout the year. If I had laid out all of those programs when I first started, it would've overwhelmed even my most committed volunteer. Instead, volunteers were able to see the need for one specific program and how their time and energy would benefit the children. Once volunteers experienced success in one program, a new idea for how children's ministry could be expanded would come to the table for exploration. Each step continues to take us closer to the big vision. And, with each small success, it's easier to buy into the big vision for children's ministry.

Josiah was thrilled when the Scriptures were uncovered in the rubble. Upon their discovery, he had a vision for all of the people he ruled to hear the words written there. They could've moaned and groaned about having to listen to the Scriptures being read, but they didn't. I have to believe that a large part of that was because they fed off of Josiah's enthusiasm. If their leader was this excited about finding the Scriptures, then there must be something exciting for them there too. First Corinthians 15:58 reads, "Be strong and immovable, always work *enthusiastically* for the Lord, for you know that nothing you do for the Lord is ever useless" (emphasis added). Your enthusiasm has to show when you are casting a vision. People have to get the message loud and clear that you are excited about children's ministry. This is not the time to sedate your emotions. Your eyes should be wide and your smile big at the very thought of how God is going to move.

Once the Ethiopian understood the truth, he was *compelled* to share what had happened to him. If that's all we know about him, then it must've been important to him. Talk with anyone and everyone who will listen about the successes you've witnessed in children's ministry. I love to tell people about the wonderful things kids say in their innocence. One child, Andrew, was four years old when he started coming to church with his mother. They had been attending for about four weeks when Andrew developed ringing in his ears. It would come and go and was more of a bother than actually hurting the little fellow. When the ringing bothered him, Andrew tugged on the ear. After about three weeks, there came a day when Andrew wouldn't stop pulling on his ear, and his mother had had enough. She said, "Andrew, I'm getting you an appointment with the doctor about that ear." He quickly replied, "Oh, no, Momma, you don't need to. I know what it is. Pastor Tina said that Jesus could speak to us and He's trying to speak to me. He just hasn't gotten on the right channel yet!" Sharing that story was a delightful way of letting people know that children were really listening and being challenged. Andrew hadn't gotten everything straight, but this comment to his mother was a great indication that he was continuing to process during the week what he had learned on Sunday.

Even in the face of negative comments or obstacles, continue to pull from deep energy resources to keep that positive picture before people. Sunday mornings, when the entire church family is gathered, there are people watching you and taking in your commitment to children's ministry. They may be people who are contemplating volunteering, grandparents who want to see their grandchildren raised in a Christian home, or people deciding where their extra finances would best be invested. Your enthusiasm needs to be ever-present for others to open themselves to the vision. I know there are days when you've got a headache or a problem is nagging at you, but let me encourage you to set those aside and let your enthusiasm leak through. It has two benefits: it speaks to those watching you and it's good medicine for your spirit.

On mornings when my arthritis is especially annoying, when I don't feel like investing in anything, I have to give myself this little lecture. *My vision is bigger than my arthritis. What do I want to show people—the person wrapped up in personal nagging challenges or someone focused and excited about what God has planned for the day?*

In order for people to catch the vision, they must already be experiencing God at work in their own lives. The passion for seeing children start their young lives with a reliance on God springs from experiencing God so real in your own life that you don't want others to miss out on what you've found. The Ethiopian eunuch changed his life when Philip communicated the gospel message, but it didn't stop there. Just as important to this biblical account is the fact that the Ethiopian man immediately had a desire to tell the rest of his countrymen about Jesus. I want kids to know that God hears and answers their prayers, because I have lived through God being available to listen to me at any hour of the day. I can look back on my life and see how God answered prayer in unique ways. I want kids to know that God cares about their situations, because I have personally experienced God's care for me. There is a richness that comes from welcoming God into everything that encompasses your life. From the joy and appreciation that is a result of witnessing, God springs the vision to raise children who will have an even richer relationship with Him.

Remember the story of the disciples who fished all night without catching any fish (Luke 5:1–7)? Jesus told them to throw the nets over the other side of the boat. When they did, the nets bulged with a multitude of fish. Jesus saw what was in the water; the disciples didn't. This wasn't an isolated incident; Jesus did this more than once. On several occasions He told the disciples to throw their nets over the other side. Even after His resurrection, He appeared on the shore and yelled out to them to once again cast their empty nets on the other side of the boat (John 21:1–6). In those words, they recognized Jesus. He used this life picture to introduce the disciples to the vision that the world is full of people waiting to be caught with God's message of salvation. Some churchgoers actually believe that they couldn't possibly be "fishers of men." They have no idea that there are children playing outside their church doors who have never heard that there is a real God who loves them more than they can imagine.

The first order of business in casting a vision is getting people to grasp the fact that there are hurting, spiritually hungry children in their communities. Raise the questions: Why should we want to reach kids? Where do we find these kids? It's easy to recognize that needy children exist in third-world countries, but to see them in our neighborhoods is a different mind-set. Ask public school teachers about the situations and needs they see in the classroom, and you'll quickly become aware that there is much work to be done. The disciples didn't see what was in the water. Let's not make the same mistake and not see the children that are only steps away from us.

When Jesus told the disciples to throw their nets over the other side of the boat, He was also telling them that in order to fill the nets they were going to have to look at things a little differently. Even though it was not their normal way to fish, there could be great benefit in changing their set ways. Let's learn from this lesson Jesus taught the disciples. In professional football, when the coach has an objection to a call, he can ask that the videotape of the questionable play be reviewed. Why? Because cameras from different angles might reveal a better picture of what actually took place. Sometimes we need a different viewpoint. Ministry may not look the way you thought it was going to look. The people who become involved on your team may not be the people you had targeted to recruit. The needs of the children you reach may need creative approaches. Be willing to throw your nets over the other side of the boat and do things a little differently.

One of the most exhilarating experiences as a leader is when you hear someone else sharing the vision that you've cast. Many things we catch aren't good for us, like the flu and poison ivy, but catching the vision enhances and changes lives, both for the one who has the vision and for those affected by it. Think of catching vision as thrust. Scientifically, *thrust* is defined as a mechanical force generated by engines to move something (such as an aircraft) forward. There are energy, desire, ideas, and passion waiting for the thrust of casting vision to be generated.

So, this is a big responsibility you have! Look at your ministry right now and think about the people you are leading. Do they know where you are headed? Is there a plan? Do people know why children's ministry is important to you? Could they tell you where you see the ministry in two years? Is your enthusiasm contagious? Are you willing to take a risk and try a new approach?

LEADERSHIP ESSENTIALS

If you are reading this book because your church is looking for someone to lead your children's ministry, the following leadership essentials can help you recognize the qualities you are looking for in a leader and can assist you in writing a job description. If you are the person who is already in a key leadership role in children's ministry, then read this as a self-evaluation. Let it point out areas where you are being successful, along with areas that you may need to address. And, if you are a member of a children's ministry team, I hope you will use this information to become an awesome team player.

Leadership Essential: Leads with a Servant Attitude

No matter what kind of leadership position you are in, it is critical to lead with a servant attitude. Let your attitude be an example to your team. As Albert Schweitzer said, "Example is not the main thing in influencing others. It is the only thing." Your team should see you work hard. They should also be confident that you're not going to ask anything of them that you're not willing to do yourself. In Mark 9:35, Jesus said, "If anyone wants to be first, he must be the very last, and the servant of all" (NIV). It's difficult to create a team atmosphere when leaders regard themselves above their teams. There are lots of inspirational and informative resources on servant leadership, so commit to learn as much as you can about what it entails.

Leadership Essential: Strives for Excellence

In all that you do, go for excellence. A word of caution though: don't confuse excellence with perfection. Without getting into a long dissertation on the difference between the two, let's simply say that *excellence* is doing the best you can with the resources you have. *Perfection*, on the other hand, is a way of doing things where there is no room for failure.

You may find yourself in less than perfect circumstances, but still be able to provide an excellent opportunity for children to be introduced to Jesus. Excellence is the perception others have of what you are doing. It's knowing that when people bring up the children's ministry at your church, it gets their stamp of quality. Every little thing is taken care of and focuses on the objective of the program. A leader either needs to be a wonderful detail person or have a close assistant who is. When details are covered, there is a flow to the event or program that has a residual effect. When things go smoothly, volunteers are happier. And when volunteers are comfortable, the children in their care get better attention. When children are cared for with excellence, parents notice. And when parents notice excellence, they want to join in.

Being average is never the goal. People won't gravitate toward mediocrity. A strong leader resists mediocrity and strives for personal and team excellence. So, go, be a river of blessing, not a puddle drying in the sun. Personally, I want to be the rapids!

Leadership Essential: Participates as a Team Player

For years I led children's ministry on my own. There were other people teaching and helping, but I hardly knew the volunteers. I maxed out on the amount of classes I could teach and programs I could lead. Over and over I sat in workshops that talked about creating a team and I couldn't imagine how that could work. Then, in an effort to prove them wrong, I decided to focus on leadership and team development. What an incredible difference it has made to my job description, in how much the children gain, in the health of the church, and in the self-esteem of the volunteers that are part of the team.

There are only a small number of people in my life that I have the ability to know intimately. That's why small groups are so important, especially in larger churches. I chose to make the volunteers on my team the small group that I know in that way. Knowing and caring for one another has resulted in the team being very close to one another. Many of my volunteers are young moms and their families now spend time together because of the bond they feel from working together in children's ministry. We go to one another for encouragement, to vent, and to share our joys. Because the friendships are strong, fear of having ideas rejected or getting negative feedback is almost nonexistent.

Developing a team spirit encourages cooperation rather than competition. You'll find that as the team develops these relationships, the volunteers will raise the bar for one another. The commitment they witness in one another keeps their own commitments strong, and they end up feeding off one another. Once, I recruited a new teacher for the first grade Sunday school class who was determined to give her classroom a new look. She wanted to make it kid-friendly and also set up for her style of teaching with learning centers. The other teachers watched and I could see the wheels of creativity turning. They saw how simple changes made huge differences. It wasn't but a few weeks and all the other classes were taking on their own personalities. Keep in mind that each time new volunteers join the team, they bring new gifts to the team and food for greater team growth. Each new volunteer presents opportunities to expand the present ministry and reach more children with higher quality programs.

The church where I minister gives me the freedom to try new things along with the freedom to fail, which was key to my development as a minister to children. As the leader of a team of volunteers, you have to give those people the freedom to experiment and if the experiment goes wrong, the freedom to fail. Help them figure out where they missed the mark, learn from it, and go on. This is big! This is where the leader of the team may have to go to bat with the board or governing body to defend an idea on behalf of the team. When volunteers can run with their ideas, there is an incredible sense of ownership that takes place along with devotion to the team—an empowering atmosphere has been created. When that happens, a climate has been successfully established where people can freely respond to what God wants them to do.

Children's ministry leaders must remember they are part of the team. All the ideas won't come from the leader. Neither does all the work come from the leader. When you're used to being completely in charge, it's a difficult transition to recognize others' ideas and trust people to carry through with the devotion you have. I can tell you though, that once that hurdle is behind you, the ministry will flourish and the opportunities will be endless. It's unbelievably rewarding.

Leadership Essential: Understands Change

Change makes most people a little uncomfortable, because it forces them to step out of their comfort zone—the places or ways that make them feel safe. In general, people love to see change in others and in other programs, but change can be difficult when it gets personal. Change means doing something in a different way, taking on new responsibilities, working alongside people you don't know that well, exposing yourself to risk, and venturing into a new investment. Those who have bought into the concept of the team and have felt supported by that group will struggle less with change, because they have witnessed the results of previous changes. They also have a track record of trust established.

Whether the change is a small one or something that impacts the entire congregation, to make it become reality, the leader has to do the research and then communicate the need and benefits of the change. Create a timeline that moves the project forward slowly but methodically and, if it's a large project, find times along the way to celebrate the progress. Changes that are made off the cuff and aren't thoroughly developed can become hazards that only create more problems.

When the leader understands why people resist change, a plan can be put together in order to tactfully and sensitively confront those issues. Let's take a look at some of the reasons for resistance to change, so you can be better prepared to encourage your team.

✿ Some people are content right where they are, doing what they have always done for years. They are comfortable with their routine and changing something may mean adjusting their schedule. Oh, I sense right now that this perfectly describes someone on your team. Sometimes you want to just say, "Get over it!" to these people, but helping them get through smaller changes first will win you an ally on larger issues. Respect their personality enough to go to them individually before the change comes up for committee discussion and approval. This simple gesture speaks volumes that you value them as a member of the team. Before mentioning what change you have in mind, create a scenario that depicts the problem. Then, give a couple of possible solutions with the positives and negatives about each. Let your enthusiasm lead the way when you speak of the change that you're hoping to institute. Ask them for input. Who knows, they may have a suggestion you hadn't thought of! Try to answer their questions and conclude by asking them if you can take this to the committee with their endorsement. If they decline, then thank them for their time and input. Share a time of prayer that, no matter the outcome of this proposal, they will continue to have a heart for children.

✿ Distrust of leadership is another reason for resisting change. Spend some time with your change-resisters to understand what might have happened in the past that contributed to this distrust. It's difficult to turn this attitude around, but intentionality is your friend. Prove yourself in small things and include the resisters in celebrating those accomplishments. One mistake new pastors or associates often make is seeing potential and making major changes before the people trust their leadership skills. If there are those with a distrust of leadership, little doses of change will ease their hesitancies.

✿ People resist change when they feel their input doesn't matter. It's easier to be positive about something when you're in the middle of what's happening and you feel your voice is being heard. Even though we can't hold them in our hands, ideas and opinions are as precious as possessions. When you're planning a change, ask for input from those who are going to play a critical part in making it happen. Be prepared to graciously affirm opinions while communicating that everything will be considered, but not everything will be used.

✿ Some people resist change because they have difficulty seeing the possibilities; they lack vision. Adults, just like children, take in information through different pathways. Telling them what your vision is may not be the right form of communication. They may need to see some kind of visual (a map, picture, or three-dimensional model). It may be beneficial to others to visit another church that is operating the program to give them the assurance that this is doable. Seeing it in motion or talking to the director provides an outside professional who lends the credibility they need.

✿ Lastly, some people resist change because they have an extremely negative nature. You know those people! The first thing that pops into their head is a reason it won't work. Consistency. That's what I have to say to you. Don't be sucked into their negativism. On my office door is a sign put out by the Siemens People Builders that says, "Negative Free Zone." I want my office to be a place known for building people up and where no idea is a bad idea. A steady diet of positivism will break even the hardest negative shell. Think of your positive outlook as drips of water dropping onto a block of ice. Eventually, drip after drip, the ice starts to break down and, one day, breaks through.

Leadership Essential: Administrates Meetings Efficiently

Although we cover more specific details about presenting a teachers' meeting in a later section, there are some basics I'll mention here. Keep your meetings positive by approaching ideas and suggestions with an explorative attitude. Respect beginning and ending times, which says to your volunteers that you respect them. Make the time set aside for the meeting a priority. By answering a cell phone or stepping out of the room to talk to someone walking down the hall, you tell the people in your meeting that they are not as important as these other little details. Prepare adequately by gathering information before the meeting and having all copies made before anyone arrives. Don't monopolize the meeting by reporting and responding to everything, but put special effort into developing your listening skills. Stay on task by keeping to the subject. Meetings usually go over the allotted time, because people are allowed to go off on tangents that do not need to be covered in the meeting. If you have difficulty moving from one item on the agenda to another, set a kitchen timer and when it goes off, that's the end of that discussion. Always end a meeting by expressing your sincere appreciation for everyone attending. There may have been some difficult issues covered, but the last words everyone hears should be words of appreciation and unity.

Leadership Essential: Sets Others Up for Success

The main job of a team leader, a children's pastor, a Christian education director, whatever that leadership position is called, is to make the volunteers successful at their part in children's ministry. Primarily, that means providing the resources they need to do the job you've asked them to do. If a teacher needs new chairs, because the ones they are presently using are pinching the children's fingers, then the leader needs to figure out how to get the chairs or make the old ones safe. If someone is building a set for the upcoming musical and needs some extra hands, then the leader needs to recruit help. If teachers and curriculum are not fitting together well, then the leader needs to look into possible alternatives in curriculum that might fit the teachers' styles better. If teachers are feeling overwhelmed at the responsibility because they are new to teaching, then arrangements need to be made for one-on-one mentoring or special training. It's a lot of troubleshooting, but solving these little issues lets the volunteers know that their leaders are willing to do anything in their power to make them shine.

Leadership Essential: Points Others to Jesus

Loggerhead turtles come out of the water onto the California beaches to lay their eggs. When the eggs finally hatch, the baby turtles instinctively move toward the sea in the dark cover of night. For many years, scientists thought the babies were moving toward the sound of the water. That all changed when the young turtles started their mad dash toward the highway that ran along the beach. What they had really been guided by was the light of the moon. Now, with the lights of the highway, they were confused about what light to use as their guide. We follow the one true light—Jesus. Other things try to outshine Him and take over as our guiding light. A children's ministry leader has to distinguish between the true and the deceptive light, constantly pointing others toward the light of Jesus. Evaluate everything as to the significance it has. Are you doing what you're doing in order to point others to Jesus?

Leadership Essential: Possesses Organizational Skills

A children's ministry leader must be able to organize people, programs, and resources without micromanaging. The ability to organize entails being able to visualize all the different parts of something and then bring them together to make the plan happen. The more leaders call upon their organizational skills in the early stages of the planning process, the easier it is to get something done with excellence (and without them losing their minds!) Someone with the gift of organization determines checkpoints in the process so that nothing gets too far off schedule or too far from the original plan. There is an infinite amount of organization that goes along with children's ministry. Without this gift, it would be almost impossible to lead, unless the job is shared with someone who does.

Leadership Essential: Motivates

Enthusiasm motivates! It's contagious! Isn't that the key to being a motivator? So turn it up a notch. Let people see your enthusiasm so they can catch the bug. People tend to take on the attitude of their leader. If the leader continually talks about how difficult situations are, then the team will take on a defeated attitude. If the leader conveys enthusiasm, even for the little things, then they'll learn to celebrate everyday moments rather than only big events. Don't store up your enthusiasm as a reaction at the end of a program's season, but let it out when you see kids smiling as they have their eyes fixed on what the teacher is about to do and say. That's a *wow* moment, so let your *wow* be heard and felt! Live with an exclamation point in everything you do.

Good leaders don't create motivation, but know how to release it in others. They know the actions and the words that excite people, inspiring them to want to be even better. Each person is filled with a treasure of valuable gifts, and a high-quality leader knows the combination of the lock that's keeping that treasure chest bolted.

Leadership Essential: Casts the Vision

We will continue to talk about casting vision for children's ministry. A necessary leadership quality is the ability to communicate that vision. A good children's ministry leader knows what children's ministry has the possibility of looking like and has the ability to make others see that picture. Not only will those people see the picture, but they will want to be involved because the leader has nurtured their desire.

Leadership Essential: Is Disciplined

Some people go in spurts, they dive into a position with all their energy. Then, one day not too long afterward, they fizzle and fade. These people aren't uncommon, and a good leader can't be someone whose commitment graph has peaks and valleys. We all have our days when we're more excited about what we're doing, but a good leader evens out that graph so the differences aren't so exaggerated. That comes through discipline. Leadership goes beyond leading when you feel good about it; good leadership is constant even when you don't feel like it.

Discipline requires someone to steadily build on what already exists, whether that is pulling a major event together, reading leadership books, or making devotional times a priority. Recognizing that big things are built out of a lot of little things is a quality that makes a great leader.

Leadership Essential: Evaluates

Not only do good leaders evaluate what they are doing, they also make sure those under them evaluate. Evaluation feels negative many times, because we think of someone else criticizing us. But serious self-evaluation increases a person's effectiveness. We'll talk about debriefing later, but a good leader needs to understand the value in constantly evaluating what is going well, what needs assistance, and what needs to be stopped.

Leadership Essential: Laughs

Don't take yourself and the ministry you have been called to so seriously that you forget to laugh. My father used to tell me that everyone needs to laugh eighteen times a day to stay healthy. I don't know where he got that number (probably made it up), but breaking the flow of things eighteen times a day can keep a person from getting too wrapped up in the intensity of present situations. People stay at a job longer when they share laughter with their colleagues. Why should it be any different with ministry partners? It's much easier to follow someone who regularly shows they have a sense of humor. Good leaders don't pass up an opportunity to lighten up.

Leadership Essential: Understands Needs

Good leadership recognizes team members' needs. Some members need to be left alone to work through things on their own. Others are so insecure that they want someone constantly reassuring them. It's critical to recognize needs such as the need to have some time off, the need to vent, or the need to be celebrated. It goes beyond being able to identify what the needs are, though. Good leaders act so that the need is met. They may not be the one to take care of a need necessarily, but they make sure it happens nonetheless.

Leadership Essential: Has a Healthy Spiritual Walk

Those in children's ministry leadership have to intentionally seek out ways to get meat in their spiritual diet. Most times everything you do is providing baby food to new or future Christians. That's not enough! A spiritual leader can't feed others when there's no food in his pantry. It's not invading someone's privacy to ask what steps they take daily to keep their spiritual walk strong and vigorous. Sincere insistence that leaders remain in a growing mode will help keep your children's ministry healthy.

I know that it sounds like a lot to find all of these leadership essentials in one person. Some qualities are most likely stronger than others, and that's okay. But the absence of any of these qualities or obvious negligence of any of them should be a warning. God has a good leader for your children's ministry, a leader who will be open to growing in every one of these areas.

PRAY-PARATION

Pray-paration is key to a complete preparation. It is the beginning, the middle, and the end of everything you attempt to accomplish. When an idea first comes to the table, listen and let God open your mind and heart to His direction. He will match people and ministry, need and provision, challenge and vision.

It's a great temptation to forego waiting and listening for God when considering a new program that has been proven successful, but it's necessary to wait for God's direction to confirm that it's part of your particular plan. Countless times I've gone to conferences and listened to pastors eloquently describe how their church had grown because they adopted a certain way of approaching ministry. The first reaction is to get charged up about going home to start the same thing. Stop. Pray.

Think. Listen. God will reveal the match between leadership, personality of the church, and your congregation's particular vision and purpose. So, first pray for the program itself.

Pray for the people who will be wearing the tool belts in the ministry; those people who will be forming relationships with kids and leading them in activities that will encourage them to process their own spirituality. In John 17:6–26, Jesus prayed for His disciples that God would keep them safe in this world and that they would grow to be more like Him. The children's ministry team should be wrapped up in prayers that they will be safe and personally grow closer to the Lord. Want to really encourage your volunteers? Write out individual prayers that you have prayed for members of your team and bless them with it as a gift.

Enlist the congregation to pray for the kids who participate in your children's ministry. As kids preregister for Bible School we always have a creative way of displaying their names in the main hallway. All children who spend at least one day with us have their names posted. After Bible School is over, members of the congregation are asked to remove names from the wall to take with them. We ask that they place these names in a prominent place in their home or office, so that they will be reminded daily to pray for that child. People can take as many names as they care to as long as they commit to pray for them. As I visit in homes or show up at workplaces, I notice the names and I praise God. Oftentimes, I will be asked at different times of the year if the child they are praying for has returned, or how they are doing. That's cause for celebration—to realize that commitments are being kept and children are being embraced in prayer even though they are quite unaware of it.

Part of pray-paration is intentionally teaching the children to pray along with the team. The commitment of the children to the ministry is vital to its health. Prayer will integrate the children into the program and help them realize their role is as necessary as anyone's. Provide the kids with a variety of ways to pray individually and corporately. Let your children hear you praying for them and for an upcoming program. Praying for children in their presence tells them they are important to you and to God. Praying for an upcoming event tells them that something important is about to happen.

Bathe your efforts in prayer and receive the assurance that you are within His plan, good and faithful servant.

GOD'S EXPECTATIONS

A Ministry of Excellence

In Malachi 1:6–8, we read how God was upset with the priests for settling for sacrifices that were less than the best. He was angry with them for offering gifts to Him that were the leftovers. (At the beginning of the Old Testament, God gave the Israelites specific instructions about what He expected of their sacrifices and offerings.) Different versions of the Bible use words like "disrespect," "insult," and "embarrass" to describe how God felt about their halfhearted offerings. They were giving better gifts to their government officials even though they claimed that God was the all-powerful One and their sovereign God. He wanted then, and wants now, the expression of our love and devotion displayed by giving the best of what we have. He doesn't ask any less of us and of our commitment to children's ministry.

God expects us to give Him our best, just as the Israelites were expected to choose their finest livestock as their offering. Therefore, our ministry should strive to be a ministry of excellence. In 1910, a company came into being that would a few years later adopt as its slogan— "When you care enough to send the very best." The company was Hallmark, a greeting card company, which to this day has a strong tradition of quality. Under the constant reminder of that motto, the employees of Hallmark are challenged to continue producing an excellent product.

Each new product is held to a high standard. Not only does God deserve our best as far as time and energy goes, but He also deserves the best quality ministry we can create. It's easy to look down on the Israelites and say, "How could they dare try get away with giving God anything but the finest piece of livestock." And yet, I can't tell you the number of times I've had someone come to me with a toy for the nursery and say, "There's only a few pieces missing and the handle doesn't work anymore, but since my kids won't play with it anymore, I thought maybe the church would like to have it." Does that sound familiar? Maybe it's just me, but it sure sounds like the Israelites who offered their crippled, blind, and sick animals. Establish the standards that will speak for your ministry and hold those standards high.

Leave It All in the Water

Our son was involved in competitive swimming for most of his life. Unlike most swimmers, Jarad's strongest part of the race was the last lap. When others were used up, Jarad poured it on. Both his coach and his father constantly drilled into his head that he needed to "leave it all in the water." Right up to that last stroke into the wall, Jarad gave all he had.

When God blesses you with the passion to minister to children, leave it all in the water. I'm not advocating that you let your priorities get out of balance, neglecting family or job. What I am advocating is that when you evaluate your ministry, you should be able to truthfully say that you didn't stop until the job was done. So when obstacles threaten to dampen your desire, you find a source of inspiration and renewal that keeps you from quitting. When there are insufficient resources, you call upon your creativity and that of others to examine every possibility. When you're short on volunteers, you see potential in everyone and find the help you need.

When I die, I hope I'm broke and used up; not a penny to my name and every ounce of energy exhausted. I'll go happily to heaven if I know that I have invested what money I had accumulated in kingdom work, totally depleted myself of the energy God had blessed me with, discovered all the ideas God had rationed for me, and left no dream unpursued.

Teach the Truth

Jesus said, "I am the way, the truth, and the life. No one can come to the Father except through me" (John 14:6). Scripture also tells us that, "the truth will set you free" (John 8:32). The truth—knowing Jesus—is what sets people free. God expects us to teach the truth in all that we do.

God gave us Scripture to be our plumb line of truth. If you're unfamiliar with a plumb line, it's a simple way of aligning something perfectly. Tie a weight on one end of a string and rub the string with chalk. Hold the end of the string against a wall and let the weight hang. It will form a perfect vertical line. (God is that line of perfection.) Then, hold both ends of the string in place against a wall, pull back the string slightly, and let go. The snap of the string will cause the chalk to make a mark on the wall. This mark reminds us of that perfect line. (The Scriptures are our reminder of God, the perfect One.) The purpose of the plumb line is to keep everything straight. If you're hanging wallpaper, the plumb line is the reference for hanging the pieces straight. If you're laying tile, the squares will only be straight if they are in correct relation to the plumb line. God expects us to stay true to the truth of the Scriptures. He expects us to use the Scriptures as our point of reference for keeping everything aligned.

Not only are we to use Scripture as our plumb line in ministry, but God expects us to teach the Scriptures as well. This is a constant battle I come up against in stocking our children's library. I insist that everything in the library be based on Scripture. There are plenty of "good" books with cute storylines about positive habits and attitudes, but kids can get that kind of reading in any library or at school. If God expects me to teach His truth, then the books in the library have to recognize His truth as their basis; they must have Scripture as their plumb line. There are lots of fun and beneficial things you can provide for kids, but your job is to provide what God expects you to—programs that promote His truth.

FORM RELATIONSHIPS

Even before the first program is discussed, there is crucial groundwork that can be laid. Start forming all kinds of relationships: with people in the congregation, the pastor, parents, organizations, people in the community not connected to the church, and kids, kids, and more kids! Take mental and written notes on each person or organization— their personalities and the skills they possess, the resources they bring to the table, the connections they may have, and how children are part of their lives. Everyone has the potential to be involved in children's ministry in some way, even if it seems trivial, such as being a supporter by placing a sign in their front yard advertising an upcoming big event.

Casual get-togethers with members of the congregation are a gold mine of opportunity to gather information. Avoid being consumed with talking about yourself, and focus on asking questions that get people to talk about what they do in their jobs and in their spare time. Did you see their eyes light up when they mentioned something they enjoy doing? They don't have to say out loud that they would be willing to help in a particular way. Their eyes say it. They probably don't even realize their talents could be of value to children's ministry. They don't know they're a truckload of possibilities. So, take the opportunity at a church function to go further than greeting someone. Invite a couple to have Sunday lunch with you. Make these occasions where you collect priceless tidbits, and also put in an excited plug for the vision you have for children's ministry. This is the perfect time to add to your never-complete file of potential supporters and workers.

Another relationship that will be vital to a successful children's ministry is the one you have with the pastoral staff. You want the senior pastor to be your number one supporter and defender. This is so imperative that I've devoted the entire next section to taking a closer look at how to approach that. In addition to the senior pastor, devote time to your relationship with the worship leader. In order for children to be incorporated into leadership in congregational worship, the worship leader needs to embrace the vision and understand the part they play in making that happen. Children will bring joy to the job of a worship leader who is open to including children. The youth pastor is also an important person to develop a healthy relationship with, because the work done in children's ministry is work done in preparation for what will be built upon later. Ask what you could do in children's ministry that would make it easier for the youth pastor to take the kids you're sending deeper and through a life-changing period of their lives. Respect his input with sincere consideration. The last thing you want to do is invest in the lives of children for ten years but then fumble as you pass them on to the youth pastor.

Pour yourself into getting to know parents, both in the congregation and outside. Find out what their felt needs are in regard to raising their children. Come right out and ask them how the church could help them be godly parents and help them bring up their children. Listen and take note of their answers and reflect on what they say as the children's ministry is put in place. It goes a long way in obtaining the support of parents when they are asked for input and then see evidence that their comments are noteworthy. Parents are very in tune with development, community activities, and the latest fun activities for kids. They have an abundance of ideas and an intense desire to see the children's ministry succeed.

Don't turn off your children's ministry radar when talking with someone outside the congregation. Even though they aren't directly connected, many times they're willing to loan or donate to the cause. When our son was in high school, we were writing a Bible School curriculum around an army theme. As I was working on it one afternoon, Jarad said, "Hey, Mom, how would you like to have a World War II Jeep?" Sure! I come to find out that the grandfather of the young man who was co-captain of the swim team with Jarad had an army jeep that was in mint condition. When we asked if we could borrow it, he didn't hesitate to say yes. After all, how in the world could kids possibly hurt a jeep that had been through World War II and survived in perfect condition? It's always worth asking, because the worst that could happen is the person could turn you down.

Find a way to connect with every kid you meet, no matter where you are. They all hold potential for participating in your church's children's ministry. Recognize one thing about each child that becomes your conversation starter whenever you see them. Those moments create a bond between the two of you, which many times can be much stronger than you realize. I keep in touch with school teachers whenever I can, as well. Knowing that I have an interest in a particular child's life, (with the parent's consent) they call on me often to provide encouragement or support. One day a teacher spoke with me about some difficulty she was having with a young man in her academically accelerated class. She had taken him to the principal that day. As they returned to the classroom after speaking with the principal, the boy looked up at her and said, "You're not going to tell Miss Tina, are you?" When she conveyed that to me, I realized that the people involved in spiritual education play a huge role in the lives of the children in their care. Don't underestimate what you mean to the children in your sphere of influence.

Relationships are built in times of great need and in times of celebration. Fight off any hesitation that you may have about making contact at these special times, because it will definitely enhance your relationship. People like to know that you are accessible and that they are being heard, so keep your ears and your heart open. Getting to know people is fun work!

SUPPORT FROM THE PULPIT

One of the key elements that you need to be assured of is the enthusiastic support of the senior pastor. Before I go any further, I'm going to admit to you that this has been fairly easy for me, since I'm married to the senior pastor. No dinner tonight if you don't support the kids! Neither threats nor bribes are really the way to go, but it is imperative that you have a plan for getting and keeping the senior pastor not only on your team but as one of the biggest cheerleaders for children's ministry. So, if you're not married to the senior pastor, what do you do? In addition to my unique relationship, I have taken other steps to educate the senior pastor about the vision for children's ministry and how it is not separate from the functioning and growth of the church body. The senior pastor must not only see the vision for children's ministry, but must embrace it. Invest some time, lots of time if necessary, to make this happen. It will be a great help when you make requests, when you present a challenging budget, or when it's not been a good week and you're in need of encouragement. Let's look at some strategies that should be included in your plan.

Be able to articulate how the purpose of children's ministry aligns with the purpose of the church. That means that you need to have a well-thought-out statement of purpose before recruiting the senior pastor's support. He needs to know that you know what you're doing and the direction you want to take the ministry. Whether you are asking for equipment to be purchased or wanting to arrange for the children's choir to sing on Sunday morning, talk about it from the point of reference of how this request will benefit the entire body of Christ. It is a difficult task to change the mind-set that "children are the church of tomorrow" to "children are the church of today." With that in mind, create opportunities where the children are integrated into key events in the church, such as a capital funds campaign or an anniversary celebration. During our capital funds campaign, the children went through a set of lessons while the pastor was preaching on the topics of the campaign. Each of the children's lessons aligned with the main point the adults were hearing. But, educating the children was not the only issue. The kids designed a "can-paign" where they collected pop cans to recycle during the entire three-year pledge period. Their receptacle for deposits was placed in an area where it would be noticed, showing that the children were also investing in the event. In addition, the kids decorated their own "First Fruits" banks from baby food jars to hold the change they accumulated. On First Fruits Sunday, the children brought in their jars and placed them in the offering plates. Each little thing like this adds to the understanding that children are part of the church *right now*.

Educate the pastor on the importance of children's ministry, but don't bombard him with statistics. All growing churches have two common characteristics: an engaging worship and a vibrant children's ministry. Let the pastor know that you are committed to children's ministry, not as a separate ministry, but to how it relates and affects the entire church. Convince him through your own enthusiasm that comes from learning and having your passion fueled. When you return from a conference, excitedly convey something you learned that speaks volumes about how important it is to the church to make reaching children a priority. The only fault he should find in you is that you are passionate beyond description!

In Henry Blackaby's book, *Experiencing God*, he makes the point that as we search for where God would have us minister, we should look for a place where we see God at work, and then join in. That always makes me think of playing jump rope as a kid. The rope is going around, and when it gets in just the right spot, you jump into the rhythm. Keep the pastor informed about what's going on in children's ministry and he'll want to jump in. The pastor is a busy person with responsibilities pulling him in all directions. Don't make the mistake of adding another thing to his hectic day by asking for half an hour to talk. Instead, as each piece of publicity, newsletter, invitation, and recruiting letter goes out, make a copy for him. Attach a Post-It note that expresses your excitement over what is happening and then put it in his mail slot. Momentum will grow as he receives one piece, then another, and another. This also builds an accountability relationship with the pastor as each piece lets him know what you're doing.

When a program is over, type up a short report that gives statistics, but also highlights the reactions of children, parents, and workers. There's no need for a long narrative or a breakdown of every item that was purchased. Just tell him how many kids were involved, how many were from outside the church, how many leaders were involved, and basically what happened. Include a positive comment you heard from a participant or worker. That's sure to sweeten his outlook on children's ministry.

Always keep in mind that the pastoral staff is a team. As much as you would like to have all the volunteer energy and budget poured into children's ministry, there are other ministries flourishing as well. Really! Keep in mind that support has a boomerang effect. When you support others, it's very likely to come back to you, but on the other hand, as others support you, be quick to cheer on the ministries they oversee. If there are times you don't understand the actions of another staff person or don't agree with how they've handled a situation, may I caution you not to succumb to the temptation to talk about it to anyone other than directly to that staff person. Division among the staff, over large or petty issues, is never a good thing. If you feel the senior pastor is not supporting children's ministry, this is no reason to pull your support of him. Look for opportunities—a statement in his sermon, the way he handles a difficult conversation, or the way he tugged affectionately on a little girl's ponytail—to point out his effectiveness and your support.

Don't make the pastor feel like he needs to be at every children's event. Choose special outreach times and let him know specifically when you need him there and what you're asking him to do. Remember, you're asking, not telling.

In many churches the senior pastor gives the announcements on Sunday morning interspersed with special announcements from other staff or laypeople. Occasionally, if there is an announcement about a children's ministry event, ask the senior pastor to give it. Make sure you've given him written information and then with a sincere smile on your face, encourage him by saying, "It's really nice when you enthusiastically support children's ministry. I appreciate it so much when you make that obvious to the congregation."

No matter how your week has gone, when it is your turn to share in a staff meeting about children's ministry, find something positive to say. It may be something that was donated, a reaction one of the kids had during an activity, a report from a parent, or how many kids are preregistered for Bible School. This positive outlook will rub off on the others, and may even have the added bonus that they will look at their own ministries in a more positive manner. It will, for sure, shine a positive light on what is happening with the kids.

When asking for permission or input from the senior pastor, approach him with as much information as you can put together. Enter the conversation with your plans in an organized manner. Imagine every question he could possibly have and try to have an educated answer prepared. This does a couple of things. It gives the senior pastor the confidence that you've thought through your proposal and it helps him see past the obstacles to the benefits.

Be quick to share the little successes, the delightful stories that identify the change happening in the lives of children. Once, when I was teaching a class of first and second graders, the final activity of the day was to create a thank you card for someone who often gets overlooked for what they do. I told them I wanted them to make sure the cards got delivered, so if they needed my help, they should just yell for me. As Rachel left, she handed me her card, and asked if I would deliver it. I smiled, and took the card to my office without opening it. When I did open it, the card read, "Dear God . . . " When I told the pastor, he got a major case of goose bumps, butterflies, and tingly sensations. Most curricula will have activity opportunities for the children to write a thank you note for someone or make a gift of appreciation. Encourage the leaders to use this part of the lesson to express their gratitude and support of the pastor. Most children see the senior pastor as bigger than life, a celebrity if you will. Let their creativity loose to come up with their own ways of expressing their thankfulness for the spiritual leadership he provides.

As I've already mentioned, work closely with the worship leader to integrate the children into congregational worship. Whether it's singing, sign language, interpretive dance, prayer, ushering, or sharing a memorized Scripture passage, children are a wonderful addition to worship. The sound of children singing automatically injects a worship service with a spirit of joy. And, listening to a child recite verse after verse of memorized Scripture makes most adults shrink in their pew from guilt and conviction.

As this topic comes to a close, I want you to think of other key leadership in your church. Some of these strategies would also be appropriate for educating them and recruiting their support. And now, the challenge is: What one thing are you going to do *today* to recruit the senior pastor as your biggest supporter and cheerleader?

PART

LAYING THE FOUNDATION

CREATING MOMENTUM

I'm always looking for an easier way to do whatever it is that I'm doing. Well, here's a riddle about something that will make your children's ministry easier. Can you guess what it is?

This is a deciding factor of growth.
It keeps people happy.
It's a lot of work to obtain, but once in the middle of it, ministry becomes much easier.
It makes recruiting easier.
It makes volunteers and professionals look much better than they are.
It is likely to inspire volunteers and professionals to become better at what they do.
It creates an incubator for change.
It makes recovery easier when something fails.
It creates more of itself.
Once started, it takes effort to stop it.
What is it?

The answer is *momentum*. Energy spent creating momentum early on will expand your ministry quickly, make recruiting easier, and make less work for you in the long run. I'll never claim to be a whiz at science, but let's take a look at what momentum is in terms of physics. One of the basic laws of physics states that an object in motion tends to remain in motion. That gets my mind whirling as I relate it to children's ministry. There's even a formula for calculating momentum: momentum equals the mass multiplied by the velocity. Now, if you're like me, I need to understand that in terms I can wrap my brain around. Mass is how much "stuff" there is, and in children's ministry let's say that is how many people and programs there are. Velocity is the speed at which that "stuff" is moving, and that would be the pace at which those people and programs are moving. You can easily see that the momentum will be greater when more people are involved and when programs are energized. This introduces us to one of the main components of creating momentum: get as many people involved as possible. Each time another person buys into the program, each time someone sees the vision, you've increased your momentum.

People willingly join in where things are happening. One of your main goals is to create a ministry that says to everyone "We're on the move!" I have a desk toy that you might be familiar with that's called a Newton's Cradle. It consists of five metal balls suspended so they are touching one another. When you pull back one of the end balls and release, it starts a motion that goes on for quite some time. When the end ball makes contact with the second ball on its downward swing, energy is sent through the other balls so that the ball at the other end reacts and is sent in motion. Back and forth the balls swing, propelling one another and being instruments of motion. Take that mental picture with you as you develop a team to work with children. What you do will cause someone else to be motivated, which in turn will motivate you more, and will draw others in. Eventually, the Newton's Cradle will come to a stop, but all it takes is for someone to pull back and release one of the end balls for the action to start all over.

Before we leave the object lesson that the Newton's Cradle offers us, let your mind hear what this toy sounds like when in motion. It's like a metronome. It has a rhythm. Clink, clink, clink, clink. When there is momentum in your children's ministry, you'll feel a rhythm. Everyone will be moving to the same heartbeat that comes from a desire to reach kids. I am not a hiker and anyone who knows me would laugh at the thought of me hiking. The other day I was in Atlanta visiting my son who is a student ministries pastor there. Jarad took his tourist parents to Kinnesaw Mountain Park to see where the battle was fought outside Atlanta during the Civil War. We parked in the parking lot and headed up a trail. When I realized that the trail was steep and it was not going to be a short walk to the top, my brain switched into its metronome mode. The beat in my head matched each footstep; there was a rhythm to my hike. That's the only way I could make it to the top. But, when I get into my metronome mode, there's no stopping to rest or investigate along the way, or I may never get started again. It's amazing how far I can walk when I synchronize my steps with the beat. Children's ministry is a rhythm you can feel. That's momentum! Keep it focused so that it's not distracted and the momentum will carry you a long way.

Heat a pot of water to 211 degrees and it's just a pot of hot water. But, take it to 212 degrees and it boils. Boiling water produces steam, which is strong enough to move a mighty engine. *One* degree! That's what made the difference. Momentum is that one degree that will create a ministry that is on the move. Cross the line from going through the motions to moving forward with momentum and you'll see your ministry doing great things and becoming a mighty engine of change.

The desire for change is why we want to experience momentum. We want to see the lives of children change, not just the children we know, but the children we've not yet been introduced to. We want to see the church change to recognize kids as important and contributing members of the family of God. When there is momentum, the congregation oozes a positive attitude, and people are happy because there is an air of success. Consequently, change is easier for them to accept. When people get on board with change, the momentum is increased. It's the Newton's Cradle again. Momentum hits at one end sending change into motion at the other end. When change returns to strike, it sends momentum into motion. The wonderful thing about this is that when momentum is created in children's ministry, it doesn't simply stay in children's ministry. It infiltrates the other ministries of the church. Whew! Isn't that exciting?

People are touched when they see God becoming a central part of kids' lives. It motivates and challenges adults to start moving to the rhythm of their own spiritual walk. Ten kids came to me one day and asked if I would help them memorize Scripture. They weren't talking about a verse here and there. They wanted to learn long passages of Scripture, even entire chapters. So, I created a program we call Lamplighters, where kids are coached on a passage, so they get to know it thoroughly as they memorize it. When they are totally prepared, our worship leader gives them the opportunity to recite the memorized Scripture in one of the worship services. It's fun to watch the adults as they listen to the scripture go on and on and on without a blink or pause from the child. The audience reacts physically. People scoot down in their pews, because they realize that kids are taking Scripture memorization more seriously than they are. And a little child shall lead them (Isa. 11:6). The momentum created within the children's ministry spills over into adult forums.

I can hear your amens, but I can also hear your questions. You want momentum, don't you? I think I've convinced you of the importance of it. But, how do you create momentum? It's easy to get charged up when you have a new idea, and it's even more exhilarating when you see that idea take form so that kids are being connected to God. If that excitement doesn't continue though, the momentum has hit a snag and is in danger of becoming stymied. Each moment of celebration needs to have another one right behind it. If you were to depict your children's ministry on a graph, you don't want it to look like mountains and valleys. You want to see a steady climbing line that is symbolic of the rhythm of you marching forward in ministry. So, let's look at some steps you can take in children's ministry that will keep you in a rhythm of momentum.

Gather Information

View each event or program as a springboard for the next one. Be an information gatherer. Use the information obtained from that program and build on it. What kind of information? Any child who attends anything the church has sponsored, no matter what it is, should be asked for information that will enable you to contact them in the future. This is a significant factor in relationship building. (We'll talk about keeping in touch with kids in a later section.) Evaluate why the kids attended and what drew them to that particular program. Understanding your "drawing" factors is valuable information. Don't wait until one program has ended before you start planning the next one. As the children complete one program, they should exit with verbal and written information about the next thing they can be involved in that has been designed specifically for them. Now, it doesn't have to be starting the next week, but the dates should be set and basic information available for the kids and parents. The message you're sending is, "We're on the move!" and "We take children's ministry seriously here."

Create the "Iwannabethere" Factor

Concentrate on attendance builders in one program. Create the "Iwannabethere" factor. Erase the notion that you can simply stand up in front of kids and say, "I'd like all of you to come back next week." Those words carry no punch, no "Iwannabethere" factor. Kids need to know *why* they should come back. They're asking themselves, "What do you have planned for me?" So, especially at first when you're establishing the "Iwannabethere" factor, lay out a plan that makes each meeting special. Some suggestions for exciting meetings:

✿ Everyone wear pajamas.

✿ Bring a sack lunch and afterward we'll all go to the courtyard to eat together.

✿ Here's a baby picture of the special guest who will be visiting. Guess who it is.

✿ Invite an adult to come to class with you.

✿ The entire class will be in candlelight one week. Don't be left in the dark!

✿ McDonald's has donated ice cream coupons. At the end of every activity, a name will be drawn to receive a free ice cream. (At the end of the day, draw out all the names that haven't been drawn and decide on a time when you can all go to McDonald's together.)

And then, promote, promote, promote!

These off-the-wall ideas tap into the "Iwannabethere" factor in kids. If you're objecting that these don't appear to have spiritual value, give me just a second. In order to teach kids lessons of spiritual significance, you have to have kids to teach! You've got to get them there first. These attendance tags create an atmosphere where you can relax and enjoy being with kids. Take advantage of these occasions to draw kids in so you can form relationships with them. Spiritual lessons can be taught while wearing pajamas. Parents do it in family devotions all the time. Teach the story of Jesus feeding the five thousand with a boy's lunch in the courtyard while enjoying the sack lunches the kids brought. The baby picture of your special guest can be someone who will share their testimony with the kids. Experience an entire lesson by candlelight focused around Jesus being the Light of the World or how we should share God's light with our dark world. The key is to let the kids know what's coming up and make them curious enough that they want to come. And, here's an extra bonus guarantee: You're going to enjoy teaching more! Let your guard down and tap into the kid who still resides inside you.

Kids, one by one, will start coming on a regular basis, because they know there's always going to be something exciting for them to do, or see, or smell, or taste, or touch. We've found that when we create the "Iwannabethere" factor in Sunday school, not only do the children's Sunday school classes blossom, but the young adult class does also. There are now people ready to learn, ready to absorb, ready to grow.

Go Public

Let it be known. Be seen. Be heard. With every little success find a way to let the congregation know about the changes taking place in children's ministry. Don't wait for the annual report to be written. Write a short enthusiastic article for the newsletter. The kids loved summer camp, so publish a booklet of the summaries they have written and pictures they have drawn of their experience there. If the church offered scholarships for camp, then post thank you notes from the kids to the church. Use the walls *outside* the classroom as a bulletin board, not just the ones inside the room, so passersby can't help but get a clue as to what is happening. Use your camera! That's my job most of the time during Sunday school. I go around to groups and classrooms taking pictures. But the pictures don't stay in my camera. They end up around doorways, as the center of construction paper flowers that adorn the baseboards, on bulletin boards, or in a display. Without fail, new pictures go up and a crowd gathers. Everyone loves looking at photographs. Each photo tells a story and sends the message, "We're on the move! Something's happening here."

Stay Focused

There are many wonderful ministries in the church, but if God has called you to children's ministry, devote yourself to it. Stay focused. As you develop a team, encourage them to keep in mind drawing others into leadership, to tweak the existing programs, and to seek God's direction for children's ministry. In the process, if you come across someone who has a desire for ministry outside the realm of children—to visit the sick or to engage with senior citizens—then pass on the word to the appropriate person who will help connect that person's gifts to a personal ministry. Stay focused on children's ministry. To create the momentum, it is going to require your concentration and intentionality. Resist being pulled away by other wonderful and relevant ministries. If God has called you to minister to children, then keep your eyes on the little ones. Renew your enthusiasm. Stay on track. The momentum will carry you forward.

Take a Field Trip

Check out other churches and how they are doing children's ministry. Talk with the leaders there. Visiting other churches can be encouraging, motivational, and inspirational. Depending on the development of your children's ministry and that of the church you're visiting, there are several different things that could happen. This could be a time when you are encouraged as you see a similar program that has been in progress longer than yours, and you see how time and perseverance has been rewarded.

Maybe you choose to visit a church that has an incredibly creative program, and what you realize is that it's doable. What they are doing isn't extravagant or pricey; it's just a new way of delivering the same message. In a conversation during this field trip you may have the opportunity to talk with someone who had a lot of experience over many years in children's ministry and you can't help but be inspired by hearing their testimony of how God has worked through kids. Let me raise this one flag of caution, though. Just because another church is doing a program and having success at it, don't mistakenly think that it is something your church needs to be doing. Check your objectives, your resources, and your volunteer base before adopting the program.

And, please, don't be threatened by what they are doing. There are plenty of kids who don't know the Lord. Let's learn from one another and make all our ministries more effective.

Promote Confidence

Find a multitude of ways to convince the volunteer staff that what they are doing is important kingdom work. They are making a difference in the lives of children and their families by investing time and energy. Appreciate volunteers both privately and publicly. Provide them with training that will motivate them to go to the next level in their leadership. When you train volunteers, the message they receive is that you think they are worthy of your investment and they must be doing something right. Can you sense how that would bring someone great joy? It makes them happy to know they are making a difference. Devote yourself to promoting confidence in them, and you'll get better leadership and less turnover because you have happy volunteers.

When there is momentum, volunteers may not be bigger than life, but their faults are less noticeable. Compliments abound, because it's part of the movement that is momentum. Everyone wants to be part of what's happening, even those who are not in children's ministry. Back to the Newton's Cradle desk toy. When people are noticed for making a contribution, they will find ways to better themselves, which just comes right back to initiate more affirmation.

Keep Moving

Create steps that are going to keep you moving forward. Write them down. Share them with your key volunteers. Be involved in several stages at once: planning, presenting, evaluating, and follow-up. Here's an example of what I'm talking about:

Forecast at the end of February

Planning: We're regularly making plans for the summer Bible Schools.

Presenting: We are in the middle of the midweek preschool program called "Make a Splash!" which will run for eight weeks.

Evaluating: We are evaluating the unit on prayer we just completed in Junior Church. We're writing up new ideas that we want to use the next time we do a similar unit.

Follow-up: Birthday cards are sent to every child on the mailing list as their birthdays come up. Families of kids who don't normally attend will receive the church newsletter as we come into the Easter season.

Can you see how there is a flow to it? It's that rhythm that we talked about earlier. Regularly check back to your objectives, your short-term and your long-term plans, because the energy that comes from gathering momentum can easily dissipate if the direction gets fuzzy.

One of the beautiful aspects of momentum is that recovery from a failure is so much easier. Momentum is created by a recent history of successes. When something doesn't go the way it was planned and the program or event registers as a failure, people tend to be less negative about it. That's because the successes significantly outweigh the failures, and recovery happens more quickly. Because momentum is created by movement, strong momentum has considerable movement behind it, which would likewise require a sizeable effort to derail it.

The Bible translation *The Message* uses the word "momentum" in two places. The first is in Acts 9:22. We see Paul at the beginning of his ministry and the Damascus believers are suspicious of him. These believers think Paul is play-acting as a believer in order to arrest them. But, Paul had been preaching, establishing his ministry, and sensed the urgency of the message. Paul had momentum and couldn't be stopped by their accusations. Early on, Paul tapped into momentum in order to launch the ministry God had given him. I challenge you to do as Paul did. Find within you such a commitment to the work God has placed in front of you that you will fight hard to create momentum that will carry you into the very heart of the ministry.

The other reference is in Matthew 4:25: "More and more people came, the momentum gathering" (MSG). The verses just before this describe Jesus healing people physically, mentally, and emotionally. Once these people were healed, they went to tell others. In turn, those people who heard of the miracles also approached Jesus. Do you feel the movement? The momentum builds. Throw yourself into ministry to children. The children you start with will communicate to others what they have learned. Their friends, their families, will come. The momentum will gather.

UNDERSTANDING CHILD DEVELOPMENT

One of my favorite television shows is "Extreme Home Makeover." In each episode a family is chosen that has a tremendous need for a new home. Many of the families chosen have special physical needs within the family and benefit greatly from having a specialized environment set up to facilitate care and therapy. Before a plan is drawn up for the home, the specific needs of the family are analyzed carefully and thoroughly. For a family who has a child with breathing problems, the home is built with a state-of-the-art air purifying system. Large open rooms, wide hallways, and low counters in the bathroom and kitchen go into a home where the mother is bound to a wheelchair. These people are able to thrive in a home created with their specific needs and capabilities in mind.

Now, compare the goal of "Extreme Home Makeover" with setting up a children's ministry. In order to create a place where children will grow and thrive spiritually, we need to understand their development stages, how they take in and process information, and what physical needs should be addressed. The list could go on and on, getting more and more specific, but let me give you some broad development characteristics for different age groups.

Two- and Three-Year-Olds

✿ They love to be on the move. Large muscles are developing more rapidly than smaller muscles. They're jumping, bouncing, running, but not yet coloring beyond a scribble.

❁ Their attention span is also on the move. Activities need to be brief, and should alternate between sitting and moving.

❁ They are starting to express themselves verbally in complete sentence structures.

❁ They like to be cuddled.

❁ They are still in the "mine!" stage. They are just beginning to understand that everything in the world is not theirs.

❁ They can learn basic biblical concepts, such as: God loves and cares about me; God made my world; and the Bible is a special book that tells me about God.

Four- and Five-Year-Olds

❁ They still love lots of movement, but small motor skills are rapidly developing. It is wise to alternate between activities that use large and small motor skills.

❁ Their attention span is still fairly short.

❁ They are curious and full of questions.

❁ They are very literal.

❁ They don't distinguish between truth and make-believe easily.

❁ They think their teachers are wonderful.

❁ They want adult approval.

❁ They start to participate in group activities.

❁ Some of the spiritual concepts they can understand: God will forgive me when I say I'm sorry for doing wrong; the Bible tells us how to live; we should obey God; we can talk to God in prayer; I have a church family that loves me; and God cares for everyone, not just me.

Grades 1 and 2

✿ Girls are generally ahead of boys in physical and intellectual development.

✿ Smaller motor skills are still developing and becoming more precise.

✿ They are expressing themselves through very simple writing.

✿ They want to do things themselves.

✿ A specific set of friends is becoming important to them.

✿ They want to please the adults in their lives.

✿ They are willing sponges for new information.

✿ They love being involved in service projects and feeling like they have made a contribution.

✿ They are ready to begin using their Bibles on their own.

✿ Spiritual concepts they can understand: Others know I am following God by my actions and words; I can understand God by seeing Him in the people around me; God is holy; God is fair and just; I am like God in some ways and different to God in some ways; God is preparing a place for me in heaven; God's way is always best.

Grades 3 and 4

✿ They are starting to establish personal identities.

✿ Their motor skills are developed to the place where they can feel successful at playing a specific sport or musical instrument.

✿ They are very aware of fairness in games, choices, and decisions.

✿ They start seeing faults in others.

✿ They have developed several very strong friendships and are somewhat protective of those circles.

✿ They like opportunities to be creative.

✿ They are able to see several viewpoints of the same issue.

✿ They are just beginning to think abstractly.

✿ Spiritual concepts they can understand: I have disappointed God by the things I have done or said; Jesus can be my personal Savior; God has a unique plan for my life; there are disciplines I can adopt that will help me grow closer to God.

Grades 5 and 6

✿ Their bodies are beginning to change.

✿ They desire to try new experiences.

✿ They are drawn toward friends and away from parents, seeking independence.

✿ They feel most comfortable with same sex activities.

✿ They start having quick mood shifts.

✿ Movie and music public figures are important to them.

✿ They start questioning what adults have told them.

❁ Spiritual concepts they understand: I can have a meaningful relationship with God; nothing exists without God; God has given me spiritual gifts.

I will be the first to admit that this is not an exhaustive list of characteristics; there's much more that could be added. And don't draw the lines between age development categories with bold, dark lines. These are generalizations and won't fit every child. Sarah, my assistant's four-year-old, hangs around with the ladies who make prayer shawls, and she can carry on a conversation that most fourth graders aren't capable of. The point is, know your kids and know where they are in their development. Tailor your curriculum and activities as much as possible to meet their developmental stage. The more age-appropriate and developmentally appropriate the activities are, the more the children will take from the experience.

When our son, Jarad, was about four years old, my sister, Tracy, was visiting our home for a few days. Something happened during that visit that awakened me to the fact that a four-year-old processes information at a different developmental level. The explanations that I thought were clear were actually quite unclear, because I used metaphors, similes, word pictures, and other abstract comparisons. One afternoon Tracy pulled out an anatomy book she was studying. Jarad was inquisitive and wanted to know what each picture was. Tracy used his questions as a personal review and patiently answered each question. "What's that?" Jarad asked. "That's the heart," Tracy responded. Jarad's eyes lit up and he said, "Oh, that's where Jesus lives!" My sister didn't know what to say. Jarad was still in a stage of development where he took everything literally. It was difficult for him to separate the physical heart from the spiritual heart. Although we may understand exactly what we mean by the words we use to represent our thoughts, young children may mis-understand because they give physical meaning to abstract concepts.

Continually work at understanding what concepts kids in different age groups are able to comprehend. This will raise questions about whether or not they should be taught the entire Bible or just parts of it. It is not important for children to be aware of all Scripture. Different parts of Scripture are more applicable to the different stages of development. Several years ago I was asked to write a couple of lessons for an editor I'd never written for and had never met. She gave me the scripture for each lesson and the first lesson was to cover Proverbs 7. Go ahead—look it up. The heading in my Bible for that chapter reads, "Warning Against the Adulteress." The editor wanted four activities for six-year-olds and four activities for upper elementary kids around this chapter! There are plenty of appropriate topics in the Bible to cover with children, I thought, so why spend time teaching something they are developmentally not ready to handle and that has no point of application relevant to their age?

In addition to considering developmental characteristics, everyone who works with children should have a basic and working understanding of *multiple intelligences*. Originally conceived by Howard Gardner (and since expanded upon), multiple intelligences is a way of understanding the different pathways the brain has at its disposal in order to take in information and problem solve. Gardner proposed that each person has seven intelligences (pathways or smarts, as some like to refer to them) and we all have an assortment of ways in which we are smart. Once people grasped this understanding and researched it further, more intelligences were suggested and, at present, there are eight that are widely accepted. It is not a matter of having some of the intelligences and none of the others; everyone has all these pathways available to them (with the exception of those with autism).

Taking a multiple intelligence inventory, though, will reveal that some of the pathways are stronger and are relied on more often. An inventory that reveals that all eight pathways are similar in strength is usually a good indicator of someone who learns quickly and efficiently. The reason is that no matter how the material is presented, they have a strong pathway processing it. Weak pathways, though, can be strengthened by exposure to new learning experiences within that pathway. Visualize a wagon wheel with eight spokes. If the spokes are different lengths, the wagon moves in a lopsided manner. If the spokes are even in length, then the wagon moves along smoothly and quickly. If someone has several very strong pathways and several that are very weak, then the way they process information is lopsided; they process some information quickly while struggling with the same concept if it is presented in a different manner. We can use our understanding of multiple intelligences to our advantage in providing a well-balanced spiritual education for our children.

Utilizing the knowledge of multiple intelligences is a great tool to reach our goal of increased understanding. Teachers and leaders need to accept the challenge of presenting material to children using as many of the multiple intelligences as possible, thereby reaching more of the target audience with the message while giving children an opportunity to strengthen their weak pathways as they are exposed to them. Before we go any further, describing the eight multiple intelligences would be beneficial. I'll refer to them, as many people do, as "smarts."

Word Smart

This is the pathway through words and is the ability to take in information and solve problems using verbal skills. Word smart encompasses being sensitive to the sounds, meanings, and even the rhythms of words. Activities that engage the word smart are: reading, writing, telling stories, and playing word games. Furnish kids with books, paper, diaries, worksheets, lectures, and an assortment of writing implements to connect with their word smart.

Math Smart

I hear you moaning! It has never failed that when I give a multiple intelligences inventory to a group, more people have math smart as their weakest smart than any other pathway. But it's not just about numbers; it's discerning in logical or numerical patterns. Experiment, question, figure out puzzles, sequence, and calculate to tap into math smart. In order to strengthen math smart, kids need to have manipulatives, codes, classifications and categories, strategic games, science paraphernalia, and exposure to museums focusing on science and space exploration. Now it doesn't sound so unapproachable, does it?

Music Smart

When someone processes information well by linking it to rhythm, pitch, or melody, they are employing their music smart. Some people will argue that music smart is the very first pathway that develops and it does so in the womb, as the baby is constantly aware of the rhythm of the mother's heartbeat. People with strong music smart love to sing, whistle, hum, tap, or listen to background music while accomplishing a multitude of other things. Music opens the door to let information come in. Find opportunities to incorporate music into Scripture memorization, story reinforcement, and games. Not only are you dishing out the music, but the kids can write their own lyrics and melodies. Years ago I had a boy come through our children's program who registered off the charts in his music smart. One week his mother consulted me about a problem he was having in his third grade studies. He could not understand how multiplication actually worked. It didn't make sense to him.

I spent one session with the boy and we put the concept to music. Each time he tried to start at square one and analyze the reasoning behind multiplication and why it works, he would sing his song and have the explanation in a language he could quickly absorb and understand. Tapping into his music smart got him over a hurdle in math.

Picture Smart

Picture smart is when information is received through the use of pictures and images. It helps with both concrete and abstract concepts. To include picture smart activities, make art, charts, movies, maps, diagrams, and puzzles. Provide a wide assortment of art supplies so they can draw, doodle, design, paint, and create. These kids appreciate trips to art museums and visual stimulation of many kinds. Have you ever gotten irritated with someone because they were doodling while you were talking? Once you understand picture smart you'll stop being upset. Doodlers doodle because it opens their pathways to listen. Since their word smart pathway doesn't want to open by merely listening to the words, doodling opens the picture smart pathway and the same information can now be received. Isn't that just incredible?

Body Smart

Gotta move! Gotta move! Gotta move! When the muscles are moving, the pathway is open. This is why hands-on activities and games are critical in children's ministry. When kids get up and use their large motor skills, the body smart pathway connects. Physical games, motions that help in Scripture memorization, crafts, "messy" activities, building, drama, and pantomime get body smart kids excited.

People Smart

People smart kids are very social and they can sense the moods of adults and other kids. Because of that understanding, they can also manipulate people to their advantage. Kids with a strong people smart are extremely relational and connect quickly through theme parties, having a mentor, being involved in the community, leadership responsibilities, and basically doing anything as long as their friends do it with them.

Self Smart

The spoke opposite people smart on our wheel is the self smart pathway. Instead of looking out, this pathway thrives on inward looking. Using self smart entails setting personal goals, meditating, spending time alone, and completing something at your own pace. Quiet reading and prayer areas encourage kids to use their self smart. We are probably guilty of neglecting the self smart pathway, because it doesn't seem very exciting. But we all need to know how to quiet ourselves and listen, so intentionally incorporate self smart activities into lesson plans. Position the kids in a circle, place a candle in the center of the room, and turn out the lights. Immediately, the children will quiet. You've created an environment for engaging the self smart pathway.

Nature Smart

This is the multiple intelligence that Gardner did not include in his original seven. We now realize that people problem solve and take in information when they connect with nature in some way. Activities that include plants or animals will fortify nature smart. Provide the kids with opportunities to classify animals and plants, take care of a class pet, go on a fishing outing together, or visit a nature center. Think about the number of times you've heard people (or yourself) testify to how they experienced God when they were out in nature. This is by far my weakest smart. When I went to camp as a teen, they had us go into the woods with our Bibles and have time alone with God. All I could think about was what was lurking behind the tree, what kind of bugs were in the log I was sitting on, and if I could find my way back. When my husband takes scenic photographs, I toss them in the garbage because my nature smart is so turned off. A friend of mine, Rick, on the other hand, can go out deer hunting and sit in a tree for hours, watching and waiting. Even if he doesn't catch anything, he'll come back saying that he had a great time. That's where he does his best thinking.

Isn't it amazing how God has wired us in such a way that we can experience His Word and His presence through many pathways? Our tendency is to teach through one or two specific pathways, and then we end up not connecting with all our kids. Teachers have to fight against the temptation to use only their strongest pathways. Kids come alive when multiple intelligences are used, because there is such a variety. Subconsciously, kids know that even if this activity is not the highlight of their day, there's something coming that they're going to get excited about. In the meantime, though, they are strengthening a weaker pathway through their participation and the spokes on that wheel are becoming just a little more even.

If kids aren't grabbing hold of what is being taught, evaluate how the multiple intelligences are being incorporated. I had my secretary make a simple sheet that has a box for each of the smarts. I use this sheet both to plan my lessons and to evaluate them. My goal is to incorporate at least five of the smarts in each lesson. That gives lots of variety and presents the lesson from different angles. If I find that one or two of the boxes are repeatedly being filled while the others are neglected, then I need to adjust some of the activities. The ones I have may be really good activities, but without addressing a wide range of smarts, you've done a disservice to the child who connects best with the pathway you chose not to use.

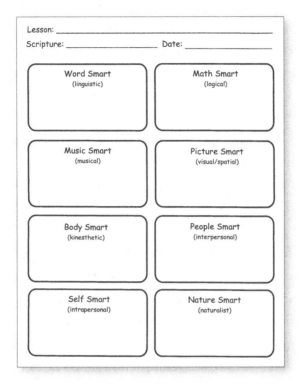

In addition to understanding multiple intelligences, familiarize yourself with the six levels of thinking from *Bloom's Taxonomy*. The most basic level of thinking is acquiring knowledge, followed by comprehension. Each level after that implies a deeper level of thinking: application, analysis, synthesis, and finally evaluation. There are certain activities that facilitate each kind of thinking. Our goal is to move children from knowing Bible stories (knowledge and comprehension) to applying them to their lives (application), and as they get older, being able to debate, make decisions, support, and defend what they have learned (analysis, synthesis, and evaluation). If we want kids to apply the biblical value taught in a certain lesson, then the activities have to support higher learning levels rather than just knowledge and comprehension. Activities that take children beyond the comprehension level are constructing and acting out scenarios, solving problems, writing down personal thoughts, creating comic strips, composing a praise song, building a model ark, and so on. As you put together your children's ministry, evaluate the level of thinking that is being asked of the students. Each time they move to a higher level of thinking the impact of the Scriptures becomes stronger.

There's one more critical area of development that needs to be discussed: a child's spiritual development. We are so anxious to lead kids through a salvation experience that we tend to misread what's really happening. I'm going to step on some toes here, but think about what I'm saying before you stomp. Children who are raised in a Christian home may feel left out if they haven't had their own spiritual experience. When they ask the first question, parents get excited and think their question is actually a statement of commitment. Remember how we listed "curiosity" as one of the characteristics of preschoolers? They ask questions, lots and lots of questions. They are naturally going to ask questions about spiritual matters. They want to find out more. Parents call me all the time and say, "My daughter asked me a question about baptism last night. When is the next baptism service so she can be baptized?" I'm amazed that they think one question of inquiry suggests they are ready for this huge step. Asking God for forgiveness, making Jesus Lord of your life, and following Him in baptism is very high-level thinking, abstract in many ways. Children don't even begin to process abstract ideas until around the third grade. Up until that point it is difficult for them to distinguish truth from make-believe on their own. Help parents understand that a personal decision to follow Christ is the most important decision a person can make and that's a lot to put on a child. Concentrate on moving them toward being a Christian and a time when that decision will be more than wanting to be like everyone else in their Christian community. Each question they ask is one more step closer to a sincere and heartfelt decision.

Your challenge is to put aside any preconceived notions of what kids are capable of and understand the truth about their development. Tap into the way God has mapped out their brains and feed them the kind of spiritual food they are able to digest at each stage.

RECRUITING AND KEEPING VOLUNTEERS

"Volunteers are unpaid, not because they are worthless
but because they are priceless!"
—Anonymous

How do you get people to volunteer and then how do you keep them doing what they promised to do? That's the cry I hear from every young children's pastor I mentor. Although the word "volunteer" denotes someone who is willingly giving time to a task, these volunteers don't come knocking on your door. Most of the time, people don't actually volunteer to take a position by coming to you and saying that they'd like to commit to be on the children's ministry team. So, how do you recruit them? Volunteers are the core of a children's ministry, so we're going to spend extra time talking about them.

Many children's pastors or directors have the idea they can run an article in the church newsletter asking for help and people will call the next day. Understand, that's a nice dream, but it's not reality. For one thing, people like to be affirmed by being asked. Many times I've approached people about helping in a certain area and they will respond with, "I was thinking that was something I'd like to do." Then, why didn't they tell me that! I'll tell you why. It's because they wanted the affirmation that I thought they would be a valuable asset in the position. We've ruled out the masses lining up at your door anxious to volunteer, so what is the plan of action for recruiting volunteers who will fill positions well? Let's look at some general steps to consider.

First of all, know the position well that you're trying to fill and then list the qualities you are looking for in a person who will fit that ministry. Maybe it's important for the position that the person be someone who will be in the classroom ten minutes before the first child arrives. As you look over the list of people you're considering, one name (Gertrude) is standing out, but Gertrude is notorious for being late to everything. In fact, the council decided to delay the starting time for Sunday school by fifteen minutes because class time was being greatly shortened due to waiting for people to arrive. (Sound familiar?) They made this change, hoping that people like Gertrude would now be there when Sunday school began. What happened? Gertrude immediately adjusted her time schedule so that she and her family arrived as late as they had before. Gertrude may be wonderful with children, but it's going to drive you bananas when every single week kids are coming to you asking what they should do because their teacher hasn't shown up yet. Use the list of qualities you pulled together to help you join a ministry with the right person. (Hold onto this list of qualities, because they'll come in handy again when you're actually talking with the person.)

When you do a jigsaw puzzle, it's a great feeling to match up two pieces and see how they fit together perfectly, how they make sense of a picture you're creating. Sometimes, out of frustration, I've been determined to force two pieces together, because I just knew I could make them work. I couldn't. The entire puzzle suffered. I added absolutely nothing to the overall picture. Caution: don't act out of desperation. A healthy church matches people with a ministry that God has called them to and it's just as important in children's ministry as anywhere else in the church. That's why running an ad in the newsletter is not a good idea. You may have one person respond whose gifts don't match and then you're left with no alternative but to fill the position with that one person.

Some basics that you look for in anyone who comes into children's ministry:

❂ They have expressed a personal faith in Jesus and are committed to their own spiritual growth.

❂ They have a heart for children. These are the people who respond with a tear or goose bumps, butterflies, and tingly sensations when you tell them about a precious comment a child made.

❂ They see children as individuals, and understand that kids aren't made with a cookie cutter or given the same personalities, desires, and preferences.

❂ They show a willingness to step out of their own comfort zones to learn new things in order to reach a child.

❂ They look at children and see possibilities, just like Jesus does.

❂ They feel an urgency and express a sense of importance in leading children to a personal relationship with their heavenly Father through Jesus.

If they have these qualities, you can train them for the rest! You're not necessarily looking for someone who has a background in education. In fact, I've found that my public educators consider what they do in their school as children's ministry and in the church they would prefer to be involved in other ministries. Challenge these professional educators, though, to be trainers and resource people. You're also not necessarily looking for people who have taught children before. These people come with predetermined ways of teaching; they come with an old set of tools. Someone who taught children in Sunday school twenty years ago will more than likely question, struggle with, and even reject methods of teaching that engage children more fully. A person who has never taught, on the other hand, will be open to learning from the ground up. When you have this raw, willing person, who is eager to be part of children's ministry, you have the opportunity to equip them to teach the way people really learn.

As you begin to form your recruiting plan, it is very helpful to understand what people are looking for—or avoiding—in a volunteer position. Your schedule is probably filled to the max with things you have to do and places you have to go, but that isn't true for many people. If you consider the time spent watching television as spare time, it is amazing how many volunteer hours are actually available. Oftentimes, the people who accomplish great things are those who are too tired, too busy, or too sick.

Followers of Christ are looking for a ministry to be involved in, not just a program. The responsibility should be big enough that it demands their attention, their input, and their committed interest. They want to know that what they are doing has an impact on the kingdom and that lives will be affected now or in the future. Volunteers want to know they are contributing to something meaningful that is worthy of their time and energy and that they are needed in fulfilling the task. You'll be glad you've cast a vision for children's ministry to the entire congregation when you start recruiting. This is one of the reasons it is so important to keep the children and what is happening within children's ministry before the congregation at all times. As we talked about in the section on pulpit support, people are much more willing to join in where they see something happening and where it is evident that God is working.

Potential volunteers want to know that if they take on a responsibility, that they will be part of a team that supports one another. Present them with the best picture possible of what they should expect. They want the assurance that they will be supported and not abandoned. Support includes a healthy amount of encouragement. One of the main responsibilities of a children's pastor is to support and encourage the children's ministry team. That means writing notes of encouragement, keeping in contact about their life situations, and dropping by when they are "in action" to give a pat on the back. Also, support means providing opportunities for development so they can more effectively do what you have asked them to do. These are all things they may have a feel for, because they have noticed the camaraderie between team members already in place and they have seen enthusiastic articles in the church newsletter that tell about training events the children's ministry team has attended. Parallel to support, volunteers like to know that they have some freedom to make the ministry their own, to add their personality and style to whatever you've asked them to do. Easy to say, but maybe not so easy to do. It may be a difficult thing for the children's pastor to let go of the idea that everything must have his or her personal mark on it.

As potential volunteers consider taking a position, they will want to know exactly what you expect of them. How much time is involved each week? Is there an ending to this commitment or a time of recommitment (in a year)? How much preparation is anticipated? Will there be a training period? Will they be expected to train others? Is there a budget for additional items or are they responsible for covering the costs themselves? Answer as many questions as you possibly can, particular to that position, and you'll find that your volunteers will stay longer and be happier, because there were fewer surprises.

When you contemplate recruiting, realize that this is not something you do in one day. It is an ongoing process; that means it never stops! Get used to the steps of recruiting so that you feel comfortable being at different stages with several people at the same time. You're developing relationships so that when the opportunity arises and you need someone to fill a position, you already have someone in mind. Recruiting should never be a crisis event. If a teacher tells you that she will be leaving her class in two months, don't wait until the class farewell party to think about who will be there next week. It should also be done in a spirit of intentionality. The plan of recruiting that I'm going to share with you has steps; it's intentional. When you call someone specifically to make a lunch appointment, they know that you have actually been thinking about them. Grabbing that person as they are passing by in the crowded hallway as church is dismissing does not convey intentionality. The person simply feels like the unlucky fish that got caught.

Begin recruiting by keeping your eyes and ears open. Enlist the rest of your team to do the same. You are capable of knowing a certain number of people. Your team members know a different sphere of people, and so the number of possibilities increases dramatically when you enlist them to help. If your team members know what you are looking for in a children's ministry worker, then their eyes and ears are as important as yours. Don't overlook anyone. And, don't be afraid to ask, even the least obvious person. You probably already have a list of reactions and excuses in your head that you're expecting, but they may surprise you.

History books tell us that in Oliver Cromwell's day there was a shortage of silver coins in the British Empire. Cromwell sent his men all over looking for silver that could be used. He even sent them to the great cathedrals looking for coins. The men reported back that there was no silver in the cathedrals, except for that which was used on the statues of the saints. Cromwell responded, "Good! We will melt down the saints and put them in circulation." It may be time to look further than the people you normally think of, maybe to the saints. Melt them down with the vision for children's ministry and put them back in circulation.

Many feel they have served their time or just don't have the energy to keep up with kids any longer, but the heart for reaching children still beats strong in them. You may have to present them with a different role than they filled in the past.

Don was a retired gentleman who taught one of the older elementary Sunday school classes. The younger kids looked forward to the day when they would get to have the white-bearded man as their teacher. Because of his carpentry skills, he built an ark with the children each year and set it afloat on the nearby reservoir with notes of encouragement aboard for whoever would find it. One day Don came to me and said that he thought he was getting too old to continue teaching. I felt strongly that God was not releasing him yet, so I simply said with a smile, "Let me know when you want to come back." He was away for a while. Then one Sunday morning, I was at my desk after the service with my back to the door and I could feel someone's presence in the doorway. For some reason I knew it was Don. I didn't turn; I just let him stand there for a long moment. When Don cleared his throat I turned to hear what he had to say. "You were right. I'm supposed to be back with those kids. God still wants me there." Don had gotten in his head that retired people aren't supposed to work with hyperactive, inquisitive kids. God told him differently.

Because you have already established a relationship with the person you're recruiting, it won't feel awkward asking them out to lunch. (I'm assuming at this point the person is of the same gender. If not, make the lunch a threesome and invite another member of your team.) I use Thursday lunch as my recruiting time. It's gotten to be a joke when my team members find out I'm having lunch with someone on Thursday. They'll make little comments that only I understand or sing lines from songs like, "Another one bites the dust." I need a rhythm in my life, so designating a special day when I do this keeps me on track. If the person you're inviting to lunch has preschoolers, provide a babysitter. That accomplishes two things: it keeps both of you focused at lunch and makes the person feel special that you've thought of this detail. Ask their preference of food and choose a nice restaurant with an atmosphere conducive to talking. McDonald's is not on the list of options! Spend the entire mealtime asking questions about their life. This is the time for them to talk and for you to initiate the lead-in questions. Get a feel for how happy they are, what problems they're having with their children, their and their spouse's satisfaction with their jobs, and so on. Catch up and develop the relationship you have already begun.

Lead the conversation into talking about how they feel about what is happening at the church. What are they excited about? If they are already involved in a ministry, how do they feel about it? Then, if you are still feeling that with all this additional information God is leading this person into children's ministry, then get more specific. Explain your vision and heart for children's ministry. Then, be very open about what you have noticed in them that makes you feel God is calling them into children's ministry at this time. Tell them what you would like for them to give prayerful consideration to and provide them with written expectations and a job description. (These are covered in another section.) This is not the time to apologize for asking them or to try to place any guilt on them if they decide against it. Point out the benefits to them personally: the fulfillment of being involved in something that has such eternal ramifications, being part of an incredible team while strengthening relationships, and the surprise benefit of learning, really learning, Bible stories. If they've already been thinking about it, their answer may come quickly. But, it's usually best to convey that you would like them to think about it for a week to make sure that the expectations match their willingness. It is imperative that you be punctual in following up on this luncheon in a week. In the meantime, you want to send them a note, thanking them for taking the time to do lunch and that you'll be praying for them as they make this decision. Oh, and by the way, you pick up the tab!

My heart began to be drawn to Jamie and the thought of her taking a key leadership position in children's ministry. Jamie was a stay-at-home mother of an eighteen-month-old energetic son. She brought several of the children in her neighborhood to Bible School and was continuously reaching out to serve them. She never hesitated to be a helper in VBS or the midweek preschool program if her schedule allowed. The children loved her warm smile and the special little touches she added to everything she did with them. Jamie had agreed to be a helper in the first-grade Sunday school class, and you could tell she was enjoying every minute of it. It gave her time to acquaint herself with the atmosphere of the class and to learn from an experienced teacher. The lead teaching position for this class was coming open. So, I asked Jamie to lunch! Several of the children's ministry team members were working in the resource room when I grabbed my purse to head out the door on a Thursday around 11:30 a.m. "Where are you going?" I heard one of them yell.

"To lunch," I replied.

"With who?"

"Jamie Smith."

Heads poked out of the doorways and together I heard dum-da-dum-dum, as if someone was walking to the gallows. They laughed and I headed out to lunch.

Jamie and I talked, we ate, and I felt strongly that she was exactly who God wanted with our first graders. I asked her if she would prayerfully consider being the lead teacher, assuring her of my support. Immediately, she looked up at me with tears in her eyes and said, "You would trust me to teach those kids?" A humbling experience for me. Wouldn't it be wonderful if everyone reacted that way, if everyone recognized the responsibility and that God was entrusting them with keeping the children's souls at such a formative time in their lives? Two and a half hours after I had left the church, I returned to cheers that another person felt the call to reach the world, one child at a time.

Let's not limit our talk of recruiting to the people who are needed for leadership positions. Extremely beneficial to a children's ministry is the support staff you recruit. These are people who have special talents that can be used to prepare crafts, fix meals, or make costumes. They are also the people you can call on to help decorate a room, paint walls, or build sets. These special volunteers are the ones who can add spice to your ministry when the leadership doesn't have the additional time to take care of these things. Find out what people like to do, capitalize on their spiritual gifts, and then make sure you call on them when you have a need they can fill. Sometimes I've even been known to create a project just so a person who has a heart for children's ministry gets the opportunity to contribute. We've developed a group called CMAs, which stands for Children's Ministry Assistants. That's exactly what they do— they assist. These are individuals who designate a certain time each week to come to the church and work on their own. I have a list of directions for all the things I need done and the supplies are there to accomplish the tasks. I like to be handy, but it isn't necessary. They mark off what they've done and leave the rest for the next CMA who comes. Each week there are odds and ends that need to be taken care of. Bulletin boards need to be changed, mailings need to be labeled, prizes need to be sorted, pieces for preschool crafts need to be cut out, goodie bags need to be packaged, shakers need to be made for the choir, and there's always lots of painting to do. Your objective is to find a place where each person can use their gifts to make a contribution to the kingdom, and for them to be happy in the process.

No matter who you are recruiting for which position, looking at their history and attitude in past volunteer positions could save you a lot of heartache. In desperate situations where you need a position filled, it is very tempting to take the first person who will say yes. For key leadership positions there are some personalities and general attitudes you want to avoid. These people types drain energy from you and your team, and become places that you are constantly trying to reinforce or work around. If these people are already in a position, you'll have to decide how you are going to deal with their attitudes in order to keep the ministry moving toward the vision. You'll recognize them:

❁ *Antiques.* These are the people who learned a method or accepted a specific translation of the Bible decades ago. They despise the thought of trying anything new, convinced that the way it has always been done is the best way. The idea of growth and what contributes to it confuses them. These are also the people who are afraid to throw anything away, even dated curriculum that was used years ago, and when asked why disposing of it would be a bad idea, they really don't know what to tell you, except that someone may need it someday. Your reaction to this person is to keep speaking positively about the vision for children's ministry. Be diligent, stubborn, and persistent on this point! Ask them to tell you what the purpose of the church is. Let's hope that some part of their answer has something to do with introducing others to Christ. Then, do your best to help them understand that making changes in teaching style or translations of the Bible (or a multitude of other changes that are continually needed) is a good thing when it means that people will be brought to a relationship with Jesus. If they have been in a leadership position with children for many years, institute some large group times where their class is merged with others and someone else is leading the activity. Speak positively of everything that happens and point out the things that the children were obviously learning. Provide them with a curriculum that makes it difficult to teach with outdated methods.

❁ *Jungle Gyms.* Some people are great with kids and love to play. Kids are attracted to them and they can easily distract crying children and put smiles on their faces, but they lack the discipline to put a lesson together. They may like the game, but won't include the debriefing time when students make sense of the activity that has just taken place. If there's time left over, they bring in a favorite fast food snack for the kids. They have won the affection of the kids, they've built a relationship, but nothing took the children closer to understanding biblical truth. These people make great helpers, but not lead teachers. Ease them into a team teaching situation where the other person will choose which activities are led by which adults. Do your best to encourage the Jungle Gyms to attend training events where they can learn how to channel those playful tendencies into learning experiences. These people can add a lot of spice and fun to your ministry, but need to be carefully placed in appropriate situations.

❁ *Whiner.* This person has a finely tuned knack for seeing the negative side of everything. No matter what is being discussed, their first reaction is to point out how it won't work and what makes it a poor idea. These people complain about the heat in their room or lack of, about an object that had been moved in their room, and about the volume of the class next door. The crazy thing is they never offer any suggestions on how something could be changed, and they just don't quit. Work at getting this person into a position that could possibly bring them an inkling of noticeable joy. Part of the whining may come from being tired of doing what they are doing, even though they don't want to admit it. Offer them some alternative positions that have a definite time period, so they know how long their commitment is. Approach them by saying that you have another responsibility that you would like for them to try and you feel may better fit their talents and gifts.

✿ *High Maintenance People.* These are the people who need your constant care. They seek your approval in everything they do. Having your input in every decision is the only way they feel safe. These people can consume a lot of your time when they could just as easily accomplish the same task on their own. First of all, you need to determine if the issue is simply a severe lack of self-esteem or if this is a persistent personality issue. If it appears to be low self-esteem, then be patient, praise them for little successes and give them tiny bits of solo responsibility where they can experience positive feedback from others, rather than just from you. Look closely at their talents and gifts so you can place them in positions where they are sure to experience success. If it is a personality trait, then do your best to redirect them to a ministry where they are meeting with one person at a time, rather than a group that has a lot of dynamics and tends to drift from the intended lesson plan. A ministry where they would accompany a veteran to visitation would give them the security that someone was there to rescue them if they said the wrong thing, but still provide them with the interaction they get when asking for your constant input.

✿ *Absentees.* These people are anxious to volunteer to go to a training event or to lead an activity group at Bible School, but at the last minute you can count on there being an excuse that keeps them from being able to follow through on their commitment. They cause embarrassment, frustration, and confusion constantly, because they refuse to follow through on what they have volunteered to do. Knowing what is more than likely to occur, you're tempted to get a substitute before you even get their call. Every time they volunteer, they do it with such heart that you want to believe that this time is different, but it never is. Approach them first to ask if they need help with their responsibility. Make an adjustment to their responsibility so that it is a team effort. Or, see if there is someone who could be a permanent substitute? Make sure the person you've recruited as their substitute understands that they may be filling the position quite often. Try to find a position where they can minister on their own time schedule or where the job would be very flexible as to when it could be done. These people want to feel part of something, they want to feel that they are contributing, but they just have a difficult time understanding the ramifications if they fail to keep their commitment.

Sometimes people aren't happy where they're serving. Here are some common reactions when people were asked why they left a volunteer position. Study them and include a plan of action that will prevent these comments being made by your team members.

✿ I felt abandoned once I took on the responsibility.

✿ It felt like a life sentence. There was no end or break.

✿ I never had the supplies I needed. It was frustrating and a financial burden to buy everything for my class.

✿ I was just filling a position.

✿ I felt like a fish out of water. One week I was sitting in an adult class, the next week I was teaching five-year-olds. There was no training.

❀ I never knew what was expected of me.

❀ It would've been nice to get a little encouragement once in a while.

Make it a personal goal to never hear these comments in your children's ministry.

Once you've got your volunteers in a position, what can you do to keep them there? Make sure your budget has made allowances for you to subsidize training events for your volunteers to attend. When they volunteer for a position, they shouldn't be expected to also foot the bill for getting their training. As much as giving them actual teaching ideas, training events are a group builder and an energizing boost. Make your training sessions or planning meetings interesting and fun, full of new ideas and social time.

Provide lots of encouragement by writing notes that speak of specific things you've noticed them doing. Take pictures of the teacher and class in action. The teacher will feel complimented that you thought the way they carried out an activity was noteworthy, and you also encourage the writers of the curriculum. Ask the teachers to e-mail you with the successes they are having in their class, so that you can share those with others at the appropriate time. While the teacher is present, point out to others something unique and creative they are doing in their class. Leave little gifts periodically for your teachers to find when they arrive in their classroom. There are books, such as *Treat 'Em Right* by Susan Cutshall or *Big Book of Volunteer Appreciation Ideas* by Joyce Tepfer that make it easy for you to add a creative card to a candy bar or other fun item to get your point across.

As you develop your volunteer base, look further down the road. Look to the future and what the team will look like in a couple of years, and then look at the older children in your ministry. If they are coming through a children's ministry that they love, they will leave with a fondness and an understanding of what a huge impact one person can have on the life of a child. Find ways to start connecting them to leadership. Once a quarter, children in our fourth and fifth grade classes go in pairs to the younger classes as student teachers. Each pair has been assigned one activity from that day's lesson that they will lead. The pair are given their assignment three weeks prior and are responsible for gathering supplies, touching base with the teacher, and presenting the activity to the class. The adult teacher is there beside them to assist and make sure the point of the activity is sufficiently communicated. These same kids are given well-defined responsibilities for helping with the younger Bible School or preschool midweek programs. This is leadership development and recruitment at the earliest stage.

The best recruiting tool is *you*. When you let your passion and excitement show 24/7; when you live to see kids learn about God; when you rub your arms and announce that you have goose bumps, butterflies, and tingly sensations because an idea sparked so many possibilities; when every conversation comes back to your love for kids . . . then you've become a walking talking billboard that says to others, "We want you for children's ministry!"

WRITING JOB DESCRIPTIONS

The thought of a job description sounds so cold and corporate, but once you get past the initial feeling that makes you bristle, you'll realize job descriptions really are a good policy to build on. The main value I have found in developing a job description for each position is that there are fewer problems to address later on. If the bar you've set is clearly defined, your volunteers will try to meet the expectations. If there is no bar of identified expectations, then no matter what they do, in their minds, they've done what they were supposed to. Job descriptions set goals and are evaluation tools. The other great value of job descriptions is that once completed, they reveal any overlap of responsibilities with other jobs and identify where something is being neglected.

If you've glanced at the next couple of pages expecting to see a set of job descriptions to work with, you're not going to find what you're looking for. The size of the church, the chain of organization, the freedom given to workers, and the number of programs are key factors that will make your church's job descriptions unique. Take, for instance, the Sunday school secretary. At the church where I now work, there is no such position. At the church we planted, there was no Sunday school. At the church we pastored in California, the church secretary kept attendance records, ordered curriculum, purchased resources, and counted the offering. At another church, the secretary took attendance and counted the offering but had no responsibility for curriculum. In smaller churches, positions have to be combined and those serving will be wearing multiple hats. The larger the church, the more specific and narrow the responsibilities. What I will give you in this section are some areas that will need thought and consideration as you write your job descriptions.

✿ Identify the spiritual gifts that would be helpful in assuming the position.

✿ How spiritually mature does the person need to be to fill this position? Is it something that someone who has not made a commitment to Christ could fill? (Preparation during the week with a small group provides a time for social interaction with believers and a feeling of contribution, but doesn't necessarily have to be done by a believer.)

✿ List personality traits that are helpful for this position. If this is for a classroom lead teacher or helper, descriptions would include: loves kids, loves to have fun, has a huge tolerance for noise, is enthusiastic, plans ahead, works well as a team member.

❀ List other qualities that apply to teaching style (if position is for a teacher). They should describe characteristics of a leader who embraces interactive, engaging learning that uses multiple intelligences; has no prior attachment to tables and pencils; has a tolerance for a confusion that leads to learning; likes variety; is receptive to change; looks at everything as a learning experience; watches for and takes advantage of teachable moments; and sticks with the main point.

❀ Specify the time commitment that is expected. If the job description is for a teacher, include class time, prep time, and the time of expected arrival and departure.

❀ Indicate expectations of attending meetings and training events.

❀ How long is the commitment? Set a beginning and ending date, at which time the person will be evaluated and asked for a recommitment. This is so helpful for recruiting volunteers. People hesitate to volunteer for something that provides no graceful way out or may never end.

❀ In addition to the age group considered and the number of children, clarify what the responsibilities will be, such as making personal contacts during the week, leading activities and discussions, being able to lead a child to Christ, teaching children how to use their Bibles, modeling Christian living both in the classroom and out, and praying for the children.

❀ Be specific about what expenses will be reimbursed and what supplies are available. Include the process for getting the reimbursements.

❀ Make it clear that personal spiritual growth is essential and you expect the person to be disciplined in their relationship with God.

Look at the words used to describe these areas above: list, clarify, expect, indicate, specify, make clear, and identify. That's because a job description should illuminate the expectations so well that the volunteer knows exactly what kind of commitment they are making. Resist watering down the job description, thinking that leaving some things out will entice volunteers to make that commitment. You'll only set yourself up for disappointment.

Once the responsibilities and expectations have been listed, take it just a little further. Most church position job descriptions don't include this, but I think it gets the relationship started with excitement and respect: list the benefits of the position! When a corporation hires a position, the applicant is told what the job entails, and what they should expect as benefits. Use your sense of humor and imagination to come up with delightful benefits. Here are a few examples:

❀ A flower picked out of a neighbor's yard wrapped in aluminum foil.

❀ Homemade construction paper cards with jelly stains on them.

❀ An invitation to a birthday party for seven-year-olds.

❀ Lots of knee hugs.

❀ A surprise visit when you're old and grey from someone in your class now, telling you how influential you were in the child's life.

❀ Witnessing *ah-ha!* moments when little eyes light up and a connection is made.

Job descriptions are a formality that, if handled correctly, can become a motivator. Take time to review the job description one-on-one with the person and share your excitement that they are willing to take on this position that will help build God's kingdom by reaching kids.

SETTING OBJECTIVES

Before any program is initiated, it should be clear to everyone involved what the objectives are. Why are we doing this? What do we want the kids to take away? Who is our target group? Is this an outreach program, or a discipleship program for the kids who already profess to be believers? Without clear objectives it's difficult to evaluate. How do you know if you accomplished what you set out to do if you don't know what the goal was? So, design the program to meet the objectives. Don't just design the program, carry it out, and then decide what objectives were met. Enter into each and every program, experience, or event with an attitude of intentionality.

If a program doesn't fit the objectives you have in mind, let someone else do it. There are a myriad of fun activities to do with kids, but do they have a purpose within the context of the kingdom of God? Is it something a club or civic group could do? If so, let them do it. Everything, and I mean everything, should somehow turn children toward God no matter how subtle the message may be. Even if the activity is mainly for fun, the way it is conducted and the attitude of the leaders should speak the Christian life. Defining objectives is so foundational that it comes even before choosing curriculum, because it is a deciding factor in that selection.

There are two main objectives that need to be decided upon for each event, experience, or program that is initiated:

1. What is the target group?

2. What decisions do you want a child to make by being involved?

Let's talk about the target group first. Here are some questions to raise, so you know who you expect to participate:

1. What age span will be involved? Is this a preschool program? An upper elementary program? Second graders? Birth through sixth grade?

2. Developmentally, where are the children? Are they toilet trained? Are they readers or nonreaders? Do they know the difference between real and make-believe? Are they entering the adolescent years? Are the children academically accelerated, do they have lower learning abilities, or a mix?

3. What socioeconomic group are the children in? Are you targeting inner-city children? Will you be dealing with unique time schedules (like farm communities or a single working parent)?

4. Will you be targeting a special group, like kids who are in day care, or those who have a special interest, such as soccer or gardening?

5. Where is your target group spiritually? Is this an outreach program where children will have their initial experience with the church, Jesus, and the Bible? Is it an educational program where children with some Bible background will be adding to their knowledge? Is it a discipleship program where children who have made a commitment to the Lord will be challenged to go deeper? Is it an event where children will experience servanthood on a personal level?

Use these questions to draw a mental picture of the children you intend to reach. Now that you have identified the target child, the next objective that needs attention is determining what decisions you want the child to make—about you, about the church, and about the Lord.

I'm going to give you six decisions that children will make consciously or subconsciously. Each one builds upon the other. You can stop at any level, but you can't skip over any decision in the order.

Decision #1: I feel safe in this place. I'm not hungry. I'm not uncomfortable. I understand my physical environment and it welcomes me. This is a place where God is honored.

Decision #2: This is a fun place to be. These people enjoy and understand kids. I don't have to act like a grown-up here. God meant for kids to have fun!

Decision #3: There are people here who care about me, because God cares about me. I have friends here. Someone knows my name and is interested in me personally. God knows my name and is interested in me.

Decision #4: I can express myself here without being put down. People here celebrate with me when I succeed and help me when I fail, because that's what God does.

Decision #5: I have seen God alive in these people, and I choose to be a believer in Jesus Christ. I will live my life with His Word as my guide.

Decision #6: I want to be a follower of Christ and grow spiritually in specific personal areas.

In order for a child to make Decision #4, he must have already made Decisions #1, #2, and #3. His self-esteem won't be healthy (#4) unless he feels safe (#1); there's an element of fun and he is respected for being a child (#2); and he has developed relationships (#3). Likewise, a salvation decision (#5) won't be made if the previous four decisions haven't been made.

If you think of children's ministry as a big picture, as a twelve-year investment from birth until promotion into the youth group, you can feel confident in setting only Decisions #1, #2, and #3 as objectives in outreach events. Bible School is one of the main places I see confusion over objectives. Churches want new families to become part of the church because of Bible School, but what takes place clearly indicates that the week is focused on children who have a strong church background. There is nothing wrong with having a Bible School for churched kids, but don't expect to attract and retain families who have never been to church. These kids have too many decisions to make in their first experience with the church.

At the beginning of our first planning meeting, we decide as a group what the objective is for presenting our two Bible Schools. These two weeks in the summer are our main outreach through children's ministry and have become the crucial growth agent for our church. Our objectives are simple. We want kids to feel comfortable in this strange environment; we want them to want to come back; and we want each child to develop a relationship with at least one adult who becomes a positive connection to the church. Is the gospel message presented? Of course! But, winning kids to Christ during the first exposure they have to His church may not be a healthy decision.

We would rather have multiple contacts with the kids in order that a sound, educated decision can be made. In short, we look for Decisions #1, #2, and #3 to be made by every child. Anything beyond that is cause for extra celebration! This is foundational work we're doing and we approach it in an extremely patient manner. Don't lose sight of the big picture, the long-range picture, where each contact with a child is simply one more building block in their spiritual growth. We're not trying to build the entire person in one week.

Objectives show up in places other than the curriculum. Think about how you're going to advertise. If your program is a discipleship program for kids who have a sound background in the Bible and have made a personal decision to follow Christ, then the church newsletter and Sunday morning announcements will be sufficient for getting the word out. But, if the objective is to reach kids who have never been through the doors of the church, then advertising takes an entirely different approach. It needs to find its way into venues where the church doesn't normally advertise. This is covered in more detail in the section on publicity.

Be clear on what the objectives are going to be before putting a program together and communicate them to the people involved. Then, stick to those objectives. Consider every element, from publicity to follow-up, to make sure it is designed to move toward that objective. Although success is difficult to measure in the church, knowing the objectives from the start makes it easier to gauge once the event is over if you accomplished what you set out to do.

IMPLEMENTING PROGRAMS

Your statement of purpose is in place, so you have a sense of the mission of your particular church. The last section gave you guidelines for determining objectives. Now, where do you start on programming?

Let's start with what you already have in place. (This section could easily be used as an outline for one of the initial meetings with your core team.) Get physical. Don't just do this in your head. Paper and pencil, dry erase board and marker, a stick and some sand. Write it down. Place each existing program into its appropriate place in your church purpose. Next to the program, write down what the target group is, as we discussed earlier. Be as specific as you can, including age group, socio-economic group, and neighborhood. Then, go back to the six decisions that were just outlined. Write down the number of the most complex decision you hope children will make in this program or event.

It's time to evaluate your ministry programs, which, of course, means answering some questions:

✿ Are all aspects of the church purpose touched on in children's ministry in an intentional manner? Is one area weighted? Is one area neglected?

✿ Are all age groups that you intend to reach provided with opportunities to participate?

✿ Are there opportunities for kids to make all six decisions? Are there a variety of decision level goals or are all goals aimed at Decision #6?

✿ Is the fun factor evident in all programs? Are children respected for the special characteristics God gave them and for their developmental stage?

✿ Which programs are working?

✿ Is any program outdated? Should it be given a dignified burial?

✿ What changes could be made to make the program fit into the purpose more effectively, to reach the target group, and to meet the decision objectives?

✿ Does the curriculum meet the needs of the program?

✿ Are the leaders pleased with the way the program is operating?

❁ Are the parents pleased with the opportunities for spiritual growth the church is offering?

If you have a children's ministry that consists of one program, perhaps Sunday school or a midweek evening program, and it has been struggling for quite some time, you have a few options. First, you could pour a lot of time, energy, and resources into trying to revive it. Or, you could scrap it all together (and probably be run out of the church if this was the very first step you took in children's ministry). Or, you could support that program, but start something completely new that is unlike anything that has been done in the past or is being done presently.

I'm advocating for option #3. Continue to recruit people called to minister to children for the existing program and offer them good training, resources, and curriculum. You want to be careful not to discredit the work that has been done for years in this venue. Then, let your enthusiasm abound as you pursue something completely new. This will create an air of excitement and anticipation with the kids and their parents. Something brand new can bring new life. It doesn't have to be a full-fledged program, but could simply be a big event. Choose something that will not compete with the objectives of the existing program. As an example, let's say that the existing program is a traditional Sunday school class with tables, chairs, printed curriculum, and take-home papers. Your splash of new programming could be:

❁ A special event where a Christian juggler is brought in to perform and share his message with the kids. This is a great opportunity for kids to bring their friends. This lends itself to some creative publicity and radio stations would willingly advertise on their community spots for something as unique as this.

❂ A new six-week program where kids are intentionally taught servanthood and given opportunities to serve their families, church, community, and the world.

❂ A Bible School that is very age-specific, perhaps to preschoolers. This is a unique way of looking at Bible School, and it will attract young families who are extremely interested in anything their little ones are a part of.

So you've decided on a direction for a new program. Great! This is your first step, but don't announce it yet. There are still some important issues to cover before promising that something is going to take place.

❂ Speak to people who have a heart for children's ministry and get their reaction to the possibility of this program.

❂ Ask: If the program was put in place, would there be people willing to commit to leading it for a designated amount of time?

❂ Find out what kind of curriculum the program will require.

❂ Consider if there is financial backing to support the entire program. Don't forget to include the cost of additional supplies, snacks, mailings, and publicity.

Once you're moving forward, present the program with excellence. Publicity should be done with as high a quality as you can afford, especially for those programs that are going to reach those outside the congregation. At the launch of the event, be totally prepared when the kids arrive. That's not saying that something unexpected won't happen, but if you're still gathering supplies when the kids and parents start arriving, you're missing out on valuable time for building relationships. The time right before and immediately following the event is critical.

Avoid letting your need to be somewhere else or procrastination rob you of these relational moments. God deserves our best, not the leftovers.

When you first start out in children's ministry, especially in a church that has little or nothing for kids, you may be tempted to start several programs at once. It's not a wise idea, because there is so much to learn, and much of it has to be learned as you go. Also, a new program takes more energy than one you've done several times before. If several new programs are starting at the same time, you'll be pulled in conflicting directions, and nothing will be given your excellent attention. So, do one thing. Do it well, and then move on. Wait for a program to get up and running. Wait for the time when you feel comfortable with how it is being led. Wait until you can go through a debriefing at the end of a unit or eight-week session. If there are major changes that need to be made, then keep waiting until you have a good grasp of how these changes can be made.

Continually return to the statement of purpose and check where the children's ministry programs fall in relation to your statement. If one area is weighted and has several programs that meet that purpose, then when another idea comes along that fits into that same purpose, justify not starting it because it will cause overload. In the same vein, if you notice an area that is lacking connection with the kids, spend time brainstorming with key leaders on the team about how to include the children.

Don't be afraid to ask kids what they like about a program and what they don't like. Use their likes and the awareness of their dislikes to your advantage. Many children's pastors today use curriculum that involves a lot of DVD presentations and videos. They have glowing reports of how their kids love it and it's easy for them to use. I thought I would try it. The first day my kids were excited about it. The next week I used it, I heard a sigh and saw that look of boredom coming on. And, the third week, they pretty much said in unison, "This again?" I've learned that my kids like a little, but not too much, when it comes to DVD curriculum. That's their group taste, and I understand. I know there are groups that the DVD appeals to and it works great. My kids love having lots of adults with them, interacting and participating in the group setting. So I recruit as many people as I can to just "hang out" during programs. You have to get to know your kids and respect their choices and preferences. The more you hit them in their sweet spot, the more successful your efforts will be.

CHOOSING CURRICULUM

The word *curriculum* may be foreign to you unless you have experience in an educational field. You also may have an incomplete understanding of it. For our purposes here, we're going to approach curriculum in two ways. First of all, let's look at curriculum as anything you use to teach your lesson. This could include the costume you wear to tell the story in the first person, the snacks the children build to mimic an object in the story, the bean bags and buckets that are used in a game, the song that relates to the story, or the video clip you watch as a class. It also includes the people who participate in teaching and dialogue. Anything that contributes to students soaking in the lesson can be classified as curriculum. Curriculum can also refer to the lesson plans that teachers use as their outlines for teaching. Each lesson has a set of activities that moves the students toward understanding as they participate in them. It tells what materials are needed, how long each activity is expected to take, and offers guidance for appropriate questions to pose. This is the meaning we are going to use for our purposes.

Let's be honest; choosing curriculum can be an overwhelming task no matter if you're just getting your feet wet in children's ministry or if you've been in it for years. The difficult part is there is such a variety to choose from now. The wonderful part is there is such a variety to choose from now! Before sitting down at your computer to view publishing company Web sites, before opening the promotional material you receive in the mail, before making phone calls or gathering input from other ministries, what should you do? First, decide on the objectives of the program you are choosing curriculum for! Write down what decisions you want the children to make. Give yourself as complete a picture as possible of how this program will fit into the statement of purpose. Then, keep these objectives close at hand as you preview and evaluate possible curriculums. Rarely do you find the perfect fit, but keeping the objectives in mind will get you as close to your goal as possible. (Are you starting to see how important a statement of purpose and objectives are?)

Most publishing companies provide samples of their curriculum for evaluation. An appendix of Web sites and company information has been included to give you a good start. More than likely, they'll provide a sample for every grade or age level you need. Larger companies will also have a variety of products that meet different objectives, such as Sunday school, Bible School, and midweek programs. These can be obtained through a request by phone or mail, or are usually downloadable at the company's Web site (see Appendix: Directory of Curriculum Publishers). Downloading samples gives you the information right when you're processing it, so you don't have to come back to it weeks later when you've finally received everything through the mail.

If the program you are starting is going to run for years, then request a scope and sequence from the company. This lays out what stories and lessons they will cover throughout a cycle. Cycles are usually two, three, or six years. That means that stories will not be repeated until the cycle is complete. A scope and sequence assures you that if the children stay connected to the program, they will get a well-rounded look at Scripture.

Here are some things to look for as you make your curriculum evaluation:

✿ Does it fit the developmental level of the children who will be involved? (Even though the curriculum is labeled for fourth grade, if most of your children have never been exposed to the Bible, then you would want to seriously consider dropping back a level or two, at least until they catch up.)

✿ Will the activities work well in your facility? (If the lessons consistently call for a large game area and you only have small classrooms, then no matter how good the activity is, you won't be able to use it.)

✿ Is there evidence of the multiple intelligences being integrated into the curriculum? (We talked about this earlier. Are there a variety of activities that touch on people, self, music, math, nature, picture, word, and body smarts? Or, does the curriculum tend to be weighted toward table, pencil and paper work?)

✿ Does the curriculum match the doctrine of your church? Check lessons on baptism, foot washing, the Holy Spirit, church membership, end times, and free will versus predestination.

✿ Will you need to purchase additional supplies? (How much are you willing to add to the budget to cover these supplies?)

✿ Does this curriculum fit into the budget? (If you lack funds, is there enough material in a lesson to use for two lessons, which would stretch the budget dollars?)

✿ Will the curriculum challenge the students by encouraging them to personalize the lessons? (Does it encourage them to take steps toward spiritual growth on their own?)

✿ Could an inexperienced teacher pick this up and understand what to do?

✿ Is it realistic to ask teachers to do the preparation that is involved with the lessons?

✿ What do your teachers think of it? (Does it challenge them to be better teachers?)

Let's look at this last item. It is imperative that your teachers like the curriculum they are asked to use. Narrow down the options by choosing curriculum that meets the objectives, then ask for input from the teachers. Give them a sample lesson to try as an opportunity to evaluate. If a teacher is asked to use a curriculum they don't approve of, the result is going to be disgruntled teaching. It will be as though a bucket of water has been thrown on the flame of enthusiasm. Although I would much rather have all my teachers using the same curriculum, at one time they had such differences in what they preferred to use, that I made the decision to use different curriculum for different grades. What we gave up in uniformity, we gained in enthusiasm. The attitude teachers have toward being with their classes is communicated whether they say the words or not, and that's your best curriculum. A happy teacher is a much better teacher, so don't overlook making a good match between curriculum and the person. After years of using multiple publishers for Sunday school curriculum, we found a curriculum that all the teachers loved and that fit our style of ministry seamlessly. The change was almost immediate. You saw the enthusiasm on the hallway walls. Kids were leaving class wearing things that related to the story, which became conversation starters with parents. Team members had changed. Not only had new teachers come onto the team, but the teachers who had been with us for a while had been trained. They now had a better understanding of child development and teaching methods. They were ignited and united. The bar had been raised. They enjoyed sharing their ideas of how they used different parts of the lesson and what they had added to it. Finding that right fit of objectives, volunteers, and curriculum propelled our Sunday school. Immediately, we saw growth in the children's classes, which caused growth in the young adult class. Keep working until you find that fit, and your entire church will benefit from it.

If nothing seems to be a good fit for your objectives and your particular church, don't be afraid to try writing your own curriculum. You know what resources you have, so you can integrate those into games and crafts. Each part of the lesson can be tailored to fit your situation perfectly. The key to writing good curriculum is to question every activity, and I mean every single activity! Does it have a strong connection to the point of the lesson? When you create a game for the children to play, is it helping them remember or understand the story or lesson point? Is the snack time connected to the story? Don't let any activity slip through your fingers and become meaningless! The incredible thing about writing your own curriculum is that there is tremendous ownership in the program that you don't get with purchased curriculum. If your entire team participates in the writing, they get great satisfaction in seeing their ideas succeed. And, if they don't begrudge the time it takes to develop curriculum, a synergy is created that adds to the momentum. Take a chance and try it. You might just fall in love with writing like I did!

CREATING EFFECTIVE LEARNING ENVIRONMENTS

Elements of a successful teaching experience include good curriculum, passionate teachers, and the resources to do the job. But one area is often overlooked, or at least put at the bottom of the "to do" list. Stand at the entrance to your classroom or learning area and put into words what message the room itself is sending you. It is very important to think first about what you have and then to create a learning environment specific to the needs of your students, one that works in conjunction with curriculum, teachers, and resources.

So what should the room say? What should the message be? When a child gets close to the room where they will be learning, there should be something outside that draws them in. Maybe it's a string of lights around the doorway or a sign that has a class picture on it. It should say, "That's me! This is where I belong!" Then, when they peek into the room, there should be cheerful colors welcoming them and interesting posters, learning centers, or places to explore, enticing them to engage. Hospital white walls are cold, harsh, and blah. (Even hospitals are now using colors on the walls to send a more comforting message to their patients.) Paint is cheap, so get out a brush and freshen up whatever space you claim as your classroom. Let me give you a few ideas from what some of my team members have done with their classrooms. We have given each class a name, and the teachers and students love to interject the characteristics of their name into the atmosphere of the room.

"The Bee-lievers" is the name of the kindergarten class. This is an interesting room because there are no walls and it's only ten feet by eleven feet. (As many as fourteen children have attended class in this little room! Far from ideal.) Two walls are accordion pleated dividers, one wall is covered with windows, and the remaining wall has the door in it with just a few feet of concrete block. That hasn't stopped the teacher from creating a room that kids love. A string of bee-shaped outdoor patio lights outline the door and are turned on when the children enter the building. The little bit of wall space is painted a sunshine yellow. A seamstress in the church made slipcovers for the chairs of yellow and black felt stripes, with a black stinger hanging down at the seat. There's a giant bee on the concrete block wall with a trail of black dashes to indicate his flight pattern. The dashes have the stories and the big idea for each lesson written on them, and each week the children add another dash to the flight. The baseboard has been painted to look like grass. Balloons made from leftover foam core hang in one corner to highlight birthdays. The cabinet door has been painted with magnetic paint, so the little laminated bees with the children's names on them will stay on the front of it.

"The Fireflies" are first graders. As you enter their room, there's a campsite set up with tent, campfire, and four foot tall skinny pine trees. The kids put a cotton ball on the end of a stick and pretend to roast it over the fire as the teacher tells the story. At the other end of the room is a rustic puppet stage where the kids can reenact stories from past lessons. Fireflies that the kids have made from toilet tissue rolls hang from the ceiling. Different tables are already outfitted with learning activities and the kids can't wait to get started.

"The Piece-makers," made up of second and third graders, use puzzle pieces as their theme. Around the doorway are bright oversized puzzle pieces, each with a child's picture and name on it. It's a large room and down both sides are giant puzzle pieces, four feet by five feet, painted in bright colors. Each one serves as its own bulletin board or learning center. There are puzzle pieces in one area to indicate birthdays. A table, called the "Lift Up" center, is set up in one corner. Each week as the kids arrive, they go to the Lift Up center to make cards for the person who is being lifted up that week. A picture of the person is there, along with a description of their need. The large metal cabinet has words from the memory verse on magnets where the kids can move the puzzle pieces around to assemble the words to make the key verse. The parts for that day's craft are already sitting on the table, raising curiosity and making the kids wonder what they're going to be doing today.

These are all rather simple touches and very inexpensive to create. More than anything, it costs time that the teacher needs to invest in thinking about the room and what it says to children the first moment they see it. The one thing I would like to caution you about is the use of murals. Although they are beautiful, they are extremely limiting. We've found that they get in the way more than they add to the room. A room that has every wall covered with the creation story is adorable and is perfect for that one lesson when you're learning about creation, but what do you do with it when you're learning about Moses leading the Israelites out of Egypt, God speaking to Samuel in the night, John baptizing Jesus, or Paul being lowered over a wall in a basket? Create learning areas around the current activity that can be adapted to any story. This leaves the room flexible as you think of new uses for it.

One of the most useful materials we have found helpful in creating environments that are easy to change is foam core insulation board. It can be purchased at any home improvement store for under ten dollars for a four foot by eight foot sheet. After removing the plastic film from both sides, project a picture from an overhead projector onto the board. Trace it and then paint it with craft paint, like you would color in a coloring book. Good colorers always outline their pictures, so outline everything with a wide black marker. Then, cut the picture out with a jigsaw using a fine blade. You'll be amazed at how good an artist you are! These figures are very lightweight and will stick to concrete block best with a removable stick-on Velcro hanger. It's loads of fun and adds so much to a room.

Challenging rooms have the possibility of becoming great learning environments for kids, but you have to do the most with what you have. Traditional ways of displaying work may not be an option, but you can hang projects from the ceiling, tape them to windows, or display them in the hallway. Use surfaces, such as the fronts of cabinets, as learning centers. The thing that draws kids into a classroom may be something that fascinates them or is mysterious. Bring in a mystery chest that holds something special for each time you meet. It may be a special prop about the story, a visiting puppet, ingredients for the snack of the day, or a map that tells the children where to go for an unexpected activity. You'll be amazed at yourself and what you can come up with!

Children need age-appropriate furnishings in their rooms. If the church doesn't want to allocate special money for a low table suitable for children, then negotiate for an adjustable table that adults can use by simply raising it. Use stackable, not folding, chairs for little ones. Too often fingers get pinched when kids lean forward and the chair shifts by folding up slightly. Preschoolers should also have easy access to bathrooms that are properly equipped for their size. Providing these furnishings tells parents that you respect the needs of their children and are concerned with their safety and comfort.

It should go without saying, but I'm going to say it anyway, that any space should be kept neat and clean. Prevent accidents, messes, and the spread of sickness by attending to the room regularly.

By taking these steps to set up an age-appropriate and engaging space, you have created a climate of growth. It will be a place where children want to be, where they are anxious to learn, and where they open themselves up to God's Word.

PROVIDING SAFETY AND SECURITY

Providing a safe environment is a basic need. Before children can accept our love or our teaching, they must feel safe. They have relied on their parents to provide that environment for them, so when they are left in our care, if they don't continue to feel safe, they'll refuse anything else we have to offer. When it comes to safety and security issues, rely on your good judgment and listen to what parents are expecting in order to feel that their child is being left in capable hands. It's almost laughable to hear about some of the ridiculous lawsuits that have been brought against organizations, until we think that something just as bizarre could happen to us. Too much time spent dwelling on the "what ifs" could leave your ministry paralyzed and too paranoid to do anything. My friend, Neil Brewer, wrote a delightful poem called "Safety First" from his collection of school memories, *The 8 O'Clock Bell*, that sums up our paranoia perfectly.

They hauled away the monkey bars,
because of Julie Brown,
She bumped her head—her mom called school—
And then they took 'em down.

The swings were really first to go,
We lost *them* 'cause of Bruce.
He walked in front of Jenna Smith,
and now his teeth are loose.

We haven't seen the merry-go-round
since Allen smashed his thumb.
His thumb got better weeks ago—
but the merry-go-round's still gone.

They banned us from the seesaw,
and I guess we all know why.
But still, we didn't know six girls
could shoot a boy that high.

So now, we're down to slidin'
just like babified beginners.
And we're not telling' *any*body
'bout these little splinters!

Prepare a policy that clarifies expectations of anyone tending to children. Run the suggested policies past a governing board for their approval, and then make them public. Post policies in the classrooms and give copies to both parents and all of your leaders. There are some basic areas that need to be addressed as you put these policies together.

Health Issues

A good frame of reference is to go to your local school administration office and ask for a copy of their policies. Keep in mind that you are not only protecting the children from one sick child, but also protecting the children from a sick adult. When are children sent home? When are children allowed to return to class? How does the school handle things like pink eye and lice? What temperature is considered a fever and a reason to remove a child from contact with others? What are the guidelines for handling blood and other bodily fluids? When are adults expected to wear gloves? How are dirty diapers, used gloves, and wipes disposed of? How often and what is the procedure for sterilizing toys? If a parent reports that their child had a communicable disease when around children earlier, how will the situation be handled?

Security Issues Involving Relationships

If you don't think this is an issue because your church is so small, then think again. One day a parent will come to you and say, "If Grandpa Ellis ever shows up to pick up Katie, she is not to go with him!" That'll send chills through you when you realize that there is someone in this child's life who is threatening her security. While a child is in your care, you are responsible to protect them from any abuse or abduction. Three important keys to avoiding any questionable situation are clear communication with parents, clear communication with leaders, and knowing your kids and their family situations well.

Complete background checks on everyone who has contact with the kids, whether they are teaching or helping, are mandatory. These can be done inexpensively, for ten dollars each, through www.protectmyministry.com. If you're not already doing this, announce a date when it will be started so that it's not a surprise to anyone. Knowing that these have been done will give parents more confidence in leaving their child in someone else's care.

Address these questions as you develop your policies. How will children be checked in and out? Where are parents expected to meet their children? When will the children be released to someone other than the people who brought them? At what point will background checks be done?

Adequate Staffing

A lone teacher is never a good idea. Another adult in the classroom provides a witness if someone questions what took place, input on how to handle difficult situations, someone to take a sick child out or retrieve a parent, extra attention to a child who needs more one-on-one attention to keep from being a distraction, and better overall teaching conditions. Keep in mind that a teenager does not take the place of an adult and is still considered a child in the eyes of the law.

In addition to background checks, make sure references are contacted. Too often these are sloughed off and applicants assume they won't be contacted. References are revealing, not only in their words, but in the tone of voice they use in describing the applicant. They will either raise caution flags or get you excited about bringing someone onto your team. Even though a prospective volunteer tells you they have been involved in children's ministry in the past, establish a waiting period before a new person to your congregation can take on responsibility. During that waiting time you or other team members will hopefully have an opportunity to get to know them on a more personal level.

Here are some questions that need consideration when preparing your policy: What are the guidelines for taking children to the bathroom? How will the class be handled if there is only one teacher available? What is the goal for the adult to child ratio? Who will check references? How long will the waiting period be before someone new to the congregation can become involved in children's ministry?

Building Safety

Some churches are utilizing very old buildings for ministry, which have a myriad of safety issues. If the church has kept up with building code regulations, the facility may be dated, but it will be safe. Familiarity may be your worst enemy on this issue. At our house there are things that need to be fixed, but we've gotten used to them and know how to work around them. The same thing happens at church. You get used to something being broken, and you cease to see it as a problem. A visitor, though, notices it as soon as they walk in a room and they immediately get the signal that their child's safety is not a priority.

Take a close look at the kind of furniture in the room, especially for smaller children. Purchase stackable chairs that are appropriately sized for the age of children using them. Avoid folding chairs that cause pinched fingers and tipping over. Adjustable tables may cost a little more, but will offer you multiuse as they can be used in the toddler classroom, as well as for adult dinners.

Your policy should also answer the following questions: Are there repairs that need to be done, no matter how minor they are? How will these needed repairs be reported? Who is responsible for making repairs? When will toys be discarded? What are the expectations of the order in which the room should be left? Are light sockets and cabinet doors equipped with child-protective devices?

Child Abuse

You are required by law to report any suspicious indicators of child abuse. Do take measures, though, to make sure you have understood the situation or meaning of the child's statement correctly. If a child says something that makes you question what has been going on at home, but you're not sure that's what they meant, ask another teacher or your supervisor to talk to the child in a similar environment as when it was initially brought up. A word of caution: words can have dual meanings. I once had a little boy who was very upset say to his leader, "My daddy beat me. He beat me bad." She came to me very concerned that the boy was being physically abused. I took him aside and asked him a few questions which revealed that his dad had been teaching him how to play checkers and "had beat him real bad." He was upset that he wasn't learning as quickly as he wanted. Take a few moments to explore what the source of the child's statement could possibly be and if that doesn't meet with your satisfaction, then you must submit an immediate report to Child Protective Services. The policy should reflect the procedure for contacting the children's pastor and senior pastor as part of the reporting process.

Establish Criteria

What are the specific steps that a children's ministry worker should take if they suspect abuse of any kind? How will records be kept, by whom, and where? Clarify that the parents, other relatives, or friends will not be contacted prior to contacting CPS. Information will not be shared with other members of the children's ministry team. State the law and adhere to it completely.

As you develop your policy for safety and security, attempt to answer every possible question that may arise. This would be a good time to conduct a brainstorming session with parents. Ask them to throw out any questions or possible scenarios that would concern them, and then make sure each one is addressed in some manner within the policies.

TACKLING DISCIPLINE

Here it is: the number one issue that volunteers and professionals want to address. When a workshop leader asks for questions about children's ministry in general, hands will go up everywhere with inquiries concerning discipline.

Discipline problems happen, and they are going to continue to happen, because we work with kids. They are exploring what is acceptable and what is unacceptable behavior. They are learning how to act and interact appropriately. They're going to mess up sometimes, and it's our job to move them to a place where they understand and assimilate the proper behavior. One of your ways of dealing with discipline problems may be that you need to remind yourself often that they are just kids and that's one of the things kids do. Although we hate to feel like the big meany, administering discipline is not evil. A healthy form of discipline promotes positive behavior. Too many people don't want to be the bad guy who sets boundaries, but kids desperately want and need boundaries. They want to know how far their behavior can safely go and discipline alerts them to when they have gone further than the boundary allows. The structure that a healthy form of discipline gives a child helps them to more clearly define who they are in relation to themselves, friends, family, and God.

Although we're going to look at causes of discipline problems and steps that can be taken to address them, the best defense is to have a good offense. Address the issue before it happens. With a good offensive plan of action, even when you have discipline problems, realize that you have prevented a myriad of them that you'll never even know about.

Understanding the causes of discipline problems can help design an appropriate offensive plan. Sometimes we look at the discipline issue being solely the child's fault. It may be something he or she is intentionally doing, but just as often if not more so, it's a reaction to something or someone around them. So, we must also look at family, teacher, and environment (classroom) as possible sources of the problem.

Students act inappropriately when they are tired. How many times have you heard a mother apologize for a whining child by saying, "They are so tired. We didn't get to bed until late last night" or "They fell asleep in the car and haven't gotten all the way awake yet"? It's difficult for me to be nice to people when my body is crying out for a nap. Why should we expect otherwise from our kids?

Some children cause problems because they're bored or overwhelmed. There isn't enough activity or the activities aren't challenging enough for them. I have one young man who is in an academically accelerated class at school, but at church he's in a class where kids have a broad range of achievement levels. He completes activities quicker than others and puts that extra time to use in inappropriate ways. On the other end of that spectrum, some kids become difficult to handle when the activity is too difficult for them. They give up and start doing something that takes little effort—becoming disruptive.

When boundaries are not adequately defined, kids can have problems. They don't know what is expected of them, or need it clarified. This may be a carry-over issue from parents. Many parents leave so many grey areas that their kids haven't quite figured out how far they can take their behavior. So, we must include poor parenting skills as the cause of discipline problems. Discipline can become an issue when kids, especially kids who don't usually cause problems, feed off one another. The child who is normally rambunctious may do something which causes another child to react. There is a chain reaction and the entire group ends up out of control. Knowing which kids ignite one another and placing them away from one another can keep this problem from occurring.

There are unexpected causes for disruptions in the class. The first break in the weather after a cold winter leaves kids wanting to be anywhere but inside. It's always a challenge on those days leading up to or following a major holiday, because the kids are distracted by their anticipation or about to burst wanting to share their holiday experience. Out-of-town guests in the home, like visiting grandparents, can keep kids wound up and their attention diverted. Another circumstance that may influence discipline problems is those times when an unexpected number of children show up, due to a holiday, special program, family reunion, or special all-church celebration.

As difficult as it may be to admit, some discipline problems are triggered by circumstances the leader has created or habits of the leader. Personally, I have found that the times when I have the most discipline problems are when I have not adequately prepared. That's why last minute substituting is so often a test of the substitute's nerves. A disorganized room gives kids permission to contribute to the disorganization by being disruptive. Children react to inconsistency in a negative way. Leaders who are sometimes playful and sometimes serious in the same type of activity are difficult to read and children often misread them. What may have been acceptable last week isn't this week. When instructions are unclear, children respond with more confusion. They act out the confusion that was initiated with the leader's lack of direction.

Recognizing that these actions on both the child's and the teacher's part can contribute to discipline issues. The question now is, "How can we aggressively take the offense to prevent issues from arising?" (As Barney Fife used to say, "You've got to nip it in the bud!")

- ✿ Pray for your kids individually. It raises their worth to you and you'll discipline differently—with more patience—when you have regularly prayed for their specific needs and spiritual growth.

- ✿ Remove the word "don't" from your discipline statements. Concentrate on replacing it with a positive way of expressing the same thing. Give the child a positive suggestion on the action you would like to see. Instead of saying with a whine in your voice, "Don't leave the table so messy," replace it with "Will you wipe the table off with this wet rag while I put the crayons in the bucket?"

- ✿ Be specific about your expectations. In the previous suggestion, the child now knows exactly what he should do—wipe the table with a wet rag. Before, he was overwhelmed with vague instructions.

- ✿ Provide lots of engaging activities. Incorporate as many of the multiple intelligences as possible in each lesson. Anticipation of what is coming next is very appealing and keeps kids on your playing field, rather than straying away to cause problems.

✿ Be prepared. When kids come through the door, everything needed for that day's lesson should be in its place. If the space is available, craft centers should be set up with everything the child needs at their seat. Time spent passing out materials is time when kids get distracted and make up their own activities.

✿ Be cheerful and wear a smile. That is very welcoming to anyone. If you find yourself getting stern when a child shows up, work on greeting the child with joy and a smile that says, "Today we are starting fresh!"

✿ Get rest. Coming into a room to face a group of enthusiastic kids calls for all the energy you can muster. Headaches make it difficult to fight off the temptation to become irritated. The main cause of headaches is the lack of good rest, and that's something you have control over.

✿ Communicate clearly what is expected—the rules and their consequences. Be consistent and carry through with the consequences that were set up initially. For persistently difficult children, talk with the parents so they understand and will, hopefully, back you up if the time comes to take firm action.

✿ Create definite cues that happen each week. During prayer time, if the children move to a specific area of the room, the actual movement will indicate that it is time to quiet down. While the children are arriving, play background music. When the music is playing they can talk with one another, but when the music is turned off, it's time to give the leader their attention. Bells, horns, lights flickering, music, motions, or moving to a particular area of the room are all good cues to establish.

❀ Provide an extra learning center for those kids who finish their work quickly and then use that extra time to be disruptive.

❀ When the weather first breaks in spring, plan an activity that can be taken outside.

❀ Anticipate when there might be an influx of kids for a session. On Sundays when Joyful Noise sings in worship, I know that our Sunday school attendance will be at its highest. Midweek, I e-mail everyone involved with the classes to remind them to prepare to be maxed out.

❀ Provide samples of all crafts. Even if directions are not completely clear to a child, the sample works as a model. Seeing a sample of the end product cuts down dramatically on questions, and when there are lots of questions, kids lose interest.

❀ Stand behind disruptive children and place your hand on their shoulders while you continue to talk. It's a very gentle way of getting their attention and your touch is a kind gesture rather than a harsh one.

❀ Whisper correction in the ear of an unruly child. Whispering conveys gentleness and patience. Just don't whisper a threat!

❀ Give semi-awake children additional time to wake up or provide a place where they can quietly rest until they are ready to participate. Very little learning will take place before they are physically ready, and sensitivity to that shows that you sincerely care.

❀ Identify extra adult help you can call upon.

❀ Involve the children in writing and posting class guidelines (rules).

✿ Keep the room neat and organized.

✿ Avoid embarrassing the child. Some children respond to correction with tears, especially kids who very seldom cause a problem. A harsh word to a tenderhearted child can bring on a flood of tears.

✿ Quiet your voice when giving instructions instead of getting louder and louder. When the children realize they're missing out on something, they'll adjust their voices to yours.

✿ Ask kids as they enter the room to make wise choices about where they sit. Say something like, "We'll all get to have more fun and participate in more of the great things I have planned if we pay attention. If there is someone here who makes it difficult for you to listen, even if it's your best friend, choose a seat where you won't be tempted to get distracted." When they make a wise choice, personally and quietly commend them on their decision.

✿ Let the children get comfortable before beginning, then make it clear that they are to stay there until the activity is over. When we move to our prayer area, the kids can lie down, sit on the floor, or pull up a chair. But once they have gotten comfortable, that is where they are asked to stay until our time of prayer is over.

✿ Ask yourself if there is something that ignites certain kids? Jerry doesn't like balloons. No matter what we are doing with balloons, he holds his hands over his ears and starts to talk loudly out of turn. He also gets disruptive whenever we do anything with food. This little boy has some special issues that trigger his negative behavior. By simply avoiding these few things, the atmosphere of the group remains constant.

❁ Be personal. The most critical time for setting the tone of the class time is as the kids arrive. If the teacher is unprepared and scurrying around to collect supplies, very personal attention that could be given to the children is neglected. This is when the kids get a chance to share their achievements, experiences, and challenges of the week, and when the teacher has the opportunity to show the childen genuine concern and care.

❁ Understand the child's home situation. This may call for some tactful conversations, but gather information about what the child faces the rest of the week. Are parents separated or divorced? Does mom work or stay at home? Is the family in a financial crisis? Is there an elderly parent being cared for in the home? Some hints on how the child is disciplined and what kind of boundaries are set will also help in dealing with future discipline issues in the class.

What if there are still problems? There are a few things I always do. One is that I let the children know that I will ask one of their parents to sit in class the following week if there are more difficult times in that day's session. Another alternative is to seek out a special helper to be that child's "buddy." It may be that they desperately need one-on-one attention. Sometimes this could even be a teenager, because the child simply needs a companion and someone to share everything with. Children act out when they have a great need for attention. They may not be getting the attention they need from school teachers or parents, and continue to ask for it in other venues by misbehaving. A buddy can go a long way in remedying this source of negative behavior. Teachers should also know that a child who becomes uncontrollable can be sent to the children's pastor for refocusing and discipline.

Provide all your workers with a discipline guide that describes actions they can take to prevent discipline problems, such as the suggestions

I've given you here. With their help, specific steps should be established as to what should be done and when parents need to be consulted about their child's behavior.

The following story sums up the feelings adults have toward discipline and the way children take it in, whether they can verbalize it this well or not. Jarad was just three years old when this happened. We were leaving church and Jarad did something that he deserved to be punished for. Daddy gave him a quick swat on the behind and strapped him into his car seat. As we were driving along with whimpers coming from the back seat, Jarad said, "Thank you, Daddy."

"What?" my husband questioned.

"Thank you, Daddy. Miss Doris (the church nursery worker), says that our parents only spank us because they love us."

Despite your views on spanking, the fact is that when discipline is administered with love, children get that message. They may not like the punishment at the time, but what they really understand is that their guardian adults care enough about them to want them to be better, to be people of God.

KEEPING IN TOUCH

Something that is often overlooked in a small to medium-sized church is the fact that you have to keep track of the kids you make contact with. If you sincerely desire to reach beyond the kids who are growing up in the church, you have to know who those unchurched kids are and make continual contact with them. Through those contacts, relationships are born. Isn't that what we're all about? Reaching kids so they can experience a relationship with Christ and His church.

I'm trying to think of a tool that is more valuable in children's ministry than the mail list, and I'm struggling to put anything above it. It's insane to think of keeping track of the kids you've had contact with without a mail list. Computer mail list programs are so inexpensive that you can't afford to be without one. They make it so easy to not only record basic information such as address, phone number, e-mail address, birthday, grade, and parents' names, but to also be able to categorize what programs each child has participated in. When I want to contact all the kids who sing with Joyful Noise children's choir, we simply edit according to Joyful Noise and all the children who have that category checked are pulled from the master list. I regularly have about one hundred kids on Sunday mornings, but there are about four hundred on my master mail list. In addition to the kid list, we develop a family mail list, because sometimes it's more appropriate to send something to the parents than the children (like at the holidays).

Obtaining the information is not difficult. We print an information card in-house, called a Kid Card (wasn't that imaginative?), which is a simple postcard ($^1/_4$ of a regular 8.5 inch by 11 inch sheet). On it we include a place for the child's name, address, zip code, phone number, age, birth date, grade, parents, who the child came with, and what programs they are attending. These cards are everywhere. Every leader has them where they can easily get to them. If we can't get all the information for the chldren, at least we obtain their names and the person they came with. Then we make a simple phone call later in the week to the people who invited them and we've got the entire card filled out. At special events, such as our Christmas Craft Day, it's very tempting for kids to pass on signing the Kid Card. We make it known that there will be door prizes handed out at the end of the event by drawing the Kid Cards, so no one wants to miss their chance to win something.

Here's what happens. One of the kids who attends church regularly brings a friend. Each time a kick-off date for any program nears, that friend receives an invitation flyer or postcard. Then, in the summer, the parents decide to send the friend to Bible School. The child has a great time, but doesn't start coming to church that next week. A flyer is sent out about the midweek program in the fall, and the child wants to attend again with their friend, but we still don't see the child regularly on Sunday mornings. One day there is a significant event in the life of the child's family: a new baby is born, someone dies, dad loses a job, or marital problems arise. Families tend to reevaluate during these times of change. The family decides that it's time to check out church and see if there's really any help or answers there. When considering where to go, the church where the kids enjoyed going as a visitor comes to mind. Very rarely do you hear of people coming to church the very first time they are asked. It takes multiple contacts before it becomes a serious consideration. Each contact you make with those unchurched kids moves them a small step closer.

It's also extremely important to stay in touch with the kids who are there every time the doors of the church are open. Kids love it when adults other than their parents recognize them as worthy of communication, whether it be through snail-mail, e-mail, or a phone call. Include postage in your budget so that you can lavish notes, cards, and announcements on the kids.

Follow-up is merely building on what you have already begun. I tell my team that if we don't publicize appropriately or follow-up efficiently, then I won't put my stamp of approval on any program or event. Let's admit it, putting a program or event together is a lot of work. But it's only part of the work. Getting the kids there (publicity) and then getting them to come back (follow-up) are also vital. Without these two, you greatly diminish the results of all the time and energy put into planning and preparing. Affirm your volunteers by letting them know that the program they are a part of is important enough to the church to spend time and money on both publicity and follow-up.

Follow-up can take many different forms, but it must be done after every event or at the conclusion of a program. If the program runs for an entire season or year, it should also be done while it's in session. Follow-up builds relationships and connections. It reminds people of who you are and what you're about, and then draws them in. It also offers your team an opportunity to really show their creativity. So, here we go. I'm going to give you some ideas on how to make those critical connections. It's far from an exhaustive list, but it'll get you started.

Holiday Mailings

We've talked about the importance of having a complete mail list, but when do you use it? There are several times during the year when we pull it out for a blanket mailing. As we approach the Christmas season we'll add all the families we have on file with the children's ministries to our normal church newsletter mailing list. December is flooded with special programs and services that people who don't normally come to church will seek out as part of their holiday celebration. So by Thanksgiving, every family we've had any connection with throughout the year will receive a mailing inviting them to attend any or all of the events planned to celebrate the birth of Christ. Usually, three mailings go out at that time. Then, again as Easter gets near, we'll do the same thing. Easter and Christmas are times when even families who do not consider the church as part of their lives will attend a service. Get the word out so they know how to join in.

Miss You

Contact kids when they've missed something they regularly attend, such as Sunday school. Don't overdo it by contacting them every time they're away, but when you notice that they've not been around for several weeks in a row, send a card or make a phone call. If no one answers, make sure you leave a message. I've actually found that kids like the messages better than talking with me. Parents report that they listen to it repeatedly and it makes them feel pretty important, since their parents are probably the only ones who ever get messages. Rather than chiding them for missing, try to keep it light. One of the fun ways of getting their attention is to write on the outside of a brown paper lunch sack "Get out of the sack and come to Sunday school!" Tri-fold the bag so the message is folded inside, and then staple it once. Address the outside of the bag with a black marker so it's easy for the postman to read, and then put a stamp on it. Yes, it will go through the mail! And, you're sure to see them the next week, giggling because of what they got in the mail from you.

Birthday Cards

Every kid on the mail list, no matter if I've only met them once, gets a birthday card from me personally. It's not a postcard but an actual card in an envelope. That's because I also send them a stick of gum as a gift. I have had the most wonderful things happen because of these cards. One little girl, Jordan, was on the mail list even though she lives an hour away and only attends Bible School when she's visiting with her grandmother. When she got her birthday card from me, she insisted that her father call me long distance so she could thank me. He tried to get around it and put it off, but she wouldn't think of continuing to celebrate her birthday until she had talked with me personally. He tracked me down on my cell phone as I was traveling in a different part of the state.

Another time, a grateful grandmother hugged me and expressed her gratitude for my remembering her grandson's birthday. The young boy's mother had been consumed with her own life and had failed to get him anything, stop by, or even call to wish him a happy birthday. That stick of gum was more than his mother offered him for his birthday.

Your mail list program will provide you with a way to pull off all the birthdays in the upcoming month. Around the 25th of each month, I get that list and make out the entire upcoming month's birthday cards. I write the birthday in pencil where the stamp will go and keep them in chronological order. Each Monday, the secretary goes through them and puts them in the appropriate mail slot so the child will receive their card as near to their birthday as possible.

Design a Brochure

Use pictures and clip art to create an attractive children's ministry brochure. Give a brief description of each program, how long it runs, where it's held, dates, times, cost, and any other information that might be helpful to an inquiring parent. We like to print our brochures in-house, which keeps the cost down tremendously. Placing an order at a printer would require large quantities. Printing in-house lets us keep the brochure current without throwing away many unused, out-of-date brochures.

We use these brochures to distribute in the follow-up packets for Bible School. They are also included in the gift bags of information and homemade cookies that are delivered to visitors. In addition, we keep a supply at our information rack and in the church office.

Recognize Achievements

When kids are involved in worship leadership—reciting a Scripture, singing, participating in a drama—make sure you follow-up with affirmation and encouragement. This past Christmas there were over sixty kids who sang in the musical that was presented as Sunday morning worship. Even though I wanted to crash that afternoon, I took the roster of the kids in Joyful Noise and I called each one individually to say something personal that I had noticed about them while I was directing. If there were siblings in the choir, I made sure that I spoke with each one. Teasha and Liesl, both five years old, still come up to me with smiles and remind me of the day when I called them.

In smaller towns, the local newspaper will often run pictures of Little League teams, kids at local carnivals, classrooms with special projects, and so on. Cut them out, highlight the name and maybe draw an arrow to point out the child, and then post it on the church news bulletin board. When it's been up for a couple of weeks, laminate it and send it to the child with a note that says "Congratulations" or "Look who I spotted!" If your church has a Web site, express personal congratulations on the kid page.

Photos

Sending pictures of kids to their parents is a great way to follow-up. Kids love to have their pictures taken and the unwritten message that parents get is, "Somebody cares enough about my kid to take a picture." Parents understand that it takes effort and time to take a picture, get it developed, design a cute frame, and actually get it postmarked. Before digital cameras, it was a common occurrence to find undeveloped rolls of film, maybe years after they were taken. We still have film of our son, taken long ago when he was a baby, that we've never viewed! With digital cameras though, there's no excuse.

To go along with every Bible School theme, we design a vignette the kids can be part of to get an individual picture taken. If they have Bible School apparel of any kind, they wear that for the photo. Also, we make sure that name tags and group logos are distinguishable in the picture for easier identification. When we used an army theme, the kids had their picture taken in a World War II Army jeep. When we used a safari theme, we borrowed a stuffed ape from the local produce market that was at least four-feet tall when it was sitting down. The kids nestled in its lap with their safari hats on and smiled for the camera. When we used a pirate theme, they stood next to a large cargo crate, draped with a fish net, and had our parrot puppet looking over their shoulder. They were adorable! We hurriedly get these developed and then post them according to the group on large posters. These are hung down the hallways, so the parents can see their child's official Bible School picture at the closing hot dog feed. Parents don't take the pictures that evening, but will receive the picture within ten days. The picture will be mounted on a card stock frame we design on the computer to go along with the theme. The full follow-up package includes the photo, a letter from me, and a brochure highlighting all the programs we offer. Each leader is given a set of address labels for the kids in their group, along with some themed postcards that have been produced in-house. They are asked to send a personal note to each of their children within the following week. And, if postage is a problem, we encourage them to drop the cards off on the secretary's desk and we'll see that they are mailed. I went to an open house this last year for a high school senior, and there was a whole display devoted to her Bible School photos—pictures for each year she participated and then for each year she helped or led a group.

Kick-Offs and Big Events

Every time a new program begins or a big event occurs, send a creative announcement to all the kids on your mail list who are eligible for it. Even if they don't attend, it keeps reminding the family that your children's ministry is active.

Computer Contacts

I am technologically challenged, but there are techy people who are interested in children's ministry and would love to use their abilities for kingdom work. Develop a children's newsletter that kids would receive periodically. It can include announcements of upcoming events and programs, congratulations, and spotlight kids, poems or stories kids have written, as well as devotionals, games, puzzles, and links to appropriate Web sites. In addition, encourage the kids to check out the kids' page on the church's Web site.

Personal Contacts

There's no substitute for a personal call, a word of encouragement or praise, or an approving touch. When you hold a metal washer close to a magnet, it is drawn to the magnet. Our words, our touch, are the force that draws kids to us, to the church, and to God. Consider yourself a magnet! When I'm in a restaurant or at the grocery, I speak to or smile at every child I see. Do you know what they do? They smile back and then they watch me until I leave their sight. If we happen to pass again on a different aisle, they're excited as though they've just noticed a friend. We connected! Sometimes that connection starts a conversation with Mom, and who knows where that'll lead. Acknowledge by name (if possible) the children you know well, and, the ones you recognize from meeting only once, whenever you're out in public. It's a great follow-up investment.

Sometimes you can pinpoint the results of following up efficiently, and other times you wonder if it's making a difference at all. When it comes to gardening, I have a black thumb, but I do have occasional success with an amaryllis bulb that was given to me. The leaves grow so quickly and I've almost given up on it some seasons, because I just about decide it's not going to produce a stem that will give me a beautiful flower. Every time I'm about to return the bulb to the garage for hibernation I notice the beginning of a little shoot of stem. I've learned to keep water-ing, even if I don't see the little shoot. Keep contacting the kids that have crossed your path. There will be results. A thorough attempt at follow-up will give you the satisfaction that you've done everything possible to connect and be available.

USING BIG EVENTS

I was standing in the parking lot, holding my glass of water, and the youth pastor who was in his vehicle getting ready to pull away was teas-ing me about something. He made one more sarcastic remark to me, and I glanced down to see that I only had half a cup of water left in my glass; there didn't seem to be a choice under the circumstances. The next thing I knew I was tossing it in his face. A little bit of water, but a big splash and lots and lots of hee-hawing! That was years ago, but we still laugh about that wet day when we see each other. The water dried up in an hour or so, but the memory lingers. That's what big events can do for your children's ministry. They make a big splash, grab people's attention, and are remembered with a smile.

Big events can be one week, one day, or one hour. What they pro-vide, especially if you have very few children in your church, is the occasion to make contacts and good memories. They are manufactured, intentional opportunities to meet children you wouldn't otherwise come in contact with. In other words, big events are strategic outreach programs. There are three things that are mandatory to making a big event worthwhile and successful: publicity, excellence, and follow-up. Since we discuss all of these in other sections, we'll move on to the sub-stance of a big event.

Big events offer your kids a wonderful opportunity to invite their friends, cousins, and neighbors. Big events should remain on the lighter side, while having some spiritual focus, so they remain fairly non-threatening. If at all possible, they should take place on your property. Just think about the last time you went to a totally unfamiliar place. It's very intimidating and you feel as though you're the only one who doesn't know their way around. At a big event, more than likely there's lots of noise, action, and interaction. Walking into that kind of atmosphere is easier, because the visitor doesn't feel as conspicuous. Also, it's easier to feel comfortable when you know that there are a lot of other kids who are having their very own first-time experience. These events are designed to be something fun that kids can share with a friend. The feelings associated with the strange place—the church—now have a positive emotion attached to them. Once you establish a track record of putting on really good events, your regular church kids will look forward to inviting their friends, because they know they can count on their friends enjoying themselves.

If the advertising is done well, and the follow-up is thorough, you'll be sending a message to the community that your church is a place where kids love to be. You're building a reputation for the church, and believe me, churches do have reputations both in the community and within their denominations. The message conveys that something is happening at your church and people like to be involved in something that is moving, growing, changing, and evolving.

One of the most exciting aspects of big events is that they can get a lot of the church involved who would normally not be engaged in children's ministry. People will volunteer for one morning, one day, or one week when they would not take on a year-long commitment. There are lots of people who I call "one shot" people. They do great pulling something together for a big bang, but shy away from commitments that would call for them to prepare something week after week or attend a regular meeting. Drawing these people in has several benefits:

✿ It gives your regular team a break.

✿ It exposes new people to the vision of children's ministry.

✿ It gives people an opportunity to explore a ministry they may not have thought they had a desire to be involved in.

✿ It's a great recruiting tool.

✿ It gives people little doses of success.

So, when you've got a big event on the calendar, look outside the group of people who you normally call upon to play key roles in both the planning and the actual event. Once, our children's choir was preparing a musical and it called for an adult to play the evil King Amon. I ran through the church directory trying to choose someone to ask, and for some reason I kept entertaining the name of a man who was a little gruff and negative toward many of the changes happening in the church. God poured a bucket of courage on me and I approached Cecil about playing the part of King Amon. The funny thing was that the kids had no preconceived ideas of what the experience with Cecil was going to be like. They just saw a man that looked like their grandpa. Within two weeks they had changed his name to "Seesaw" and Cecil melted. Not long after that he went into my husband's office (the senior pastor) and said that he was beginning to understand why we had to reach outside of our congregation and leave our comfort zones. He's not been involved in children's ministry since that one musical, but he's a solid supporter of what we do for kids and consistently expresses a positive attitude that we can now count on. Because Seesaw had been such a "pillar" in the church for decades, his change in attitude was contagious. It was one of the smartest things I ever did, and I'm so thankful for the direction God gave me. Cecil was exposed to the children's ministry vision through a big event.

Let me just tickle your thoughts with a few ideas that we, or friends of mine, have used for big events:

❀ *Angel Breakfast.* We had an intergenerational breakfast with a heavenly theme as part of our Easter celebration. The Resurrection Angel came to tell the story of Jesus' resurrection from His unique point of view. Other churches have done a similar type of breakfast as part of their Christmas activities.

❀ *A Special Act.* We had Jesse the Juggler come to entertain the kids with his juggling talents. Each part of Jesse's routine related to a biblical message.

❀ *Lunch and a Movie.* I invite all the kids who are not going out of town on spring break to bring their friends to share lunch and a movie with me. Lunch is hot dogs, chips, and Rice Krispie treats. The kids are encouraged to bring a blanket and pillow and we sack out on the floor to watch a G-rated movie we project onto the largest plain wall we can find.

❀ *Christmas Craft Day.* The week following Thanksgiving we provide a Christmas Craft Day, where for two hours kids travel from station to station at their own speed to prepare twelve different crafts that become part of their holiday celebration. Parents are invited to share the experience with their children and take plenty of pictures.

❀ *Little League Day.* We invited all the Little League teams to come to church in uniform. They sat together during worship and both the teams and coaches were recognized by the pastor. Afterward, there was a hot dog lunch, along with lots of silly "baseball" games that everyone could get involved in.

❀ *Theme Days.* Take one thing, like water, bananas, or a particular culture (like Mexican), and create a big event where everything is connected to that theme.

Big events are fun! They're fun to plan, fun to participate in, and it's fun to see the results!

USING A BUDGET

Budgeting is tedious, stressful, and absolutely necessary. This is where you have to submit to being over-the-top accountable. The best advice I can give about budgeting is to give more information in your budget than anyone would ever dream of asking for.

The first time a budget was requested of me, the committee asked for a lump sum. I threw it out at them and I thought there were going to be multiple heart attacks. Lump sum makes it extremely difficult, because the finance committee sees this huge number and immediately wants to draw its sword to defend the offering plates. I shrunk under their scrutiny, and truthfully, felt like I had done something wrong. And I had. I had not been prepared to show them exactly how the money was being invested in ministry. So, I immediately started keeping records of all expenses and what each program or need cost. I now have twenty-six categories (or line items) to break down the children's ministry costs. Included are categories for each of the sixteen programs, teacher appreciation, training, bulletin boards, decorations, publicity, supplies, subscriptions, resources, new equipment, and postage. It's easy to overlook details when you're trying to remember every expense of putting a program together that happened eight months ago. You can inadvertently ask for too little because a certain aspect of the program didn't cross your mind.

You can never gather too much information. Every second you spend preparing for your budget requests is time well spent. Slay the dragon of defensiveness and get on the offense. Justify each category without being asked by reporting how many children were reached and how many were from outside the church. Report any new volunteers you may have pulled in to assist in the program. Linking people with a ministry is a huge positive that normally isn't taken into account when looking at the benefits of a program. Let your excitement for what is going on show through the words you use to describe each category. Give examples of what parents, kids, or workers have said about the program. If Sarah's mom told you that Sarah asks each morning if it's the day for "Make a Splash!" (the preschool midweek program), then add that comment with that category justification. Express how kids felt about being involved and how it drew them or their family closer to the Lord. Were there families that came to the church directly or indirectly related to children's ministry? And, to lighten the moment, throw in a few funny things that kids have said throughout the year. These are things the committee wants and needs to know. It's your job to convince them that money put into children's ministry is good stewardship.

If you are requesting more money than last year, then tell why it is needed. Are you hoping to reach more children, which translates into more individual supplies? Did you use up leftover supplies in last year's session and will have to purchase new ones this year? Did someone make a large donation toward the program last year that you can't count on again? Have you used old curriculum in the past and need to purchase new? Do you want to try something new or go a different direction with the program?

Finish your budget request by stating the vision you have for children's ministry. What are your short range (the next year) and your long range (five- to ten-year) plans? The committee will be impressed by your thoroughness and your forethought. A well-researched budget presentation sends the message that you know what you're doing and you're not going to be careless with the funds that are entrusted to you.

Other than the actual budget presentation, there are a few things that help to get the stamp of approval from the finance committee. Kids represent hope for the future. They give adults the confidence that the ministry they have invested their lives in will continue. So, kids need to be seen often throughout the year—serving, leading in worship, and participating. There also needs to be visual evidence that something is going on. Are you displaying the kids' projects in the hallways where everyone can see them? Are there pictures of the kids in action on the bulletin board? Does the church have a different feel because there are children present? This way, the committee already has a positive outlook on children's ministry and the part it plays in your particular church.

I'm not saying that if you do these things you'll get everything you ask for, but it will make even a church on a tight budget think seriously about how they are investing the funds that are their responsibility.

In a church that is struggling financially, especially in the first few years when the church might not have completely embraced children's minstry yet, you may have to figure out ways to support it outside the church budget. For several years I spent as much time fundraising as I did working with kids. We delivered ten thousand phone books in order to offer Bible School in a local park. I put together so many yard sales that I don't care to ever go to another one. But I did it, because I believed that there were kids in our community that God wanted to place in our care. That's part of helping the church see the importance of reaching kids. When they see that you're willing to do anything to make it happen, others will join you, and they will support it financially. Now, in the words of every mother, "Have you done your homework?"

PART

FRAMING

PUBLICITY

Regularly, I see and hear about wonderful programs that a church has put together, and then my heart sinks when I ask them how they publicized the event. I am especially disheartened when I find out that it was intended to be an outreach to unchurched kids. Don't overlook publicity! A lot of work is poured into preparing lesson plans, gathering supplies for crafts, preparing for snacks, games, and music. Each child who attends is precious, but wouldn't it be more gratifying to have the rooms full and the hallways buzzing? What an encouragement to leaders to know that someone thinks so much of what they are planning that there is an actual plan of attack for publicizing it! This bears repeating, and I repeatedly tell my team, "If we're not going to bother to advertise or follow-up, then let's not do all the work of putting this together."

We've talked about the critical element of having objectives, and a very important objective is your publicity. If your objective is to reach children who have grown up at the church, then the forms of publicity used within the church are sufficient. Take advantage of the church newsletter, bulletins, and PowerPoint announcements. If it's something really special, then a short, clever skit at the beginning of the service will get everyone's attention. These are fairly traditional means of publicity. A sign-up sheet in the children's wing might be appropriate, as well as a postcard reminder of the starting date. Don't assume that everyone read or heard the announcement if it's only given once. Churchgoers are just as absent-minded as other people and need to be reminded, even of the things they are looking forward to and supposedly have on their calendars.

Events that are meant to reach into the community to attract kids who have never gone to church or are currently not attending, demand creative publicity. We'll give you some ideas here, but there are ways unique to your community, so you'll want to keep your eyes and ears open. As parents register their kids for a program, don't be afraid to ask them how they heard about it. Keep track of your findings and study them. You'll be able to tell what means of advertising effectively connected with people and convinced them to give this a try. On the other hand, it will help you eliminate methods of advertising that showed no return for your investment. Make wise use of the budget allotted for advertising, so you can get the most for your money.

Word of mouth will inevitably be the best way to get the word out. Knowing that, come up with different tools that can be placed in the hands of people in the congregation, which make it easier for them to open their mouths.

If the children are presenting a musical, provide them with packets of invitations that have been made specifically for that musical. Invitations can be printed in-house on a computer printer, but produce them as professionally as you can with the resources you have. Each invitation should include a place where children can sign their names to personalize it. Encourage the children to take enough to mail or pass out to their classmates, neighbors, relatives, ball teams, karate clubs, and even scouting groups. During the Christmas season, they can be included in the family's Christmas cards.

Produce a door hanger that members of the congregation can pass out in their neighborhoods. Put the information on one side and a registration blank on the back. As the people walk through their neighborhood on an evening stroll, the door hanger will be a conversation starter. Assemble a team of students to hand them out in the neighborhood surrounding the church and in neighborhoods largely inhabited by young families. Caution those delivering door hangers to attach them sufficiently, so they're not seen blowing around the yards later that day.

Some youth ball fields sell space for advertising on their outfield fences or by the concession stand. Ball fields are made up entirely of families, the exact group you are targeting. We've found the rates are very reasonable and many times they make the signs for you. Each time someone goes for a hot dog or drink, they're reminded of your event. During each game, over and over, their eye surveys the signs where your message is stationed. Many times, the ballparks will also give permission to post flyers on telephone poles or other support poles.

Consider a contest to encourage kids to ask their friends. When we were planning our farm-themed Bible School, we talked the senior pastor into participating in our contest. If we had 150 kids preregistered by the Sunday prior to Bible School beginning, the pastor agreed to eat a chicken dinner on the roof of the church. We had 151 before church let out, and the congregation gathered outside to enjoy the pastor sitting on a blanket on the slanted roof, chomping on a chicken leg. To make sure he ate the entire dinner there, someone removed the ladder!

For several weeks before a big event that children need to register for, include a registration form in each bulletin. This not only makes it convenient for members of the church to register their own children, but it gives them a registration to take to a child they have on their mind to invite.

This may seem like one of those ideas that's way out there, but I'll use it as an example in order to give you permission to think beyond the traditional methods. When we were using an international theme, we had fortune cookies made. Instead of a fortune, though, each cookie included a slip of paper giving dates and times of the event. People in the church were encouraged to take a supply of the cookies and pass them out at the grocery, in the mall, at a team practice, or wherever they might run into a parent with kids in tow. It created opportunities for conversation and personal contact. Made-to-order fortune cookies can be purchased online at very reasonable rates.

Most churches purchase the lawn sign that goes along with the Bible School material they are using. These are generally small, fragile, and don't draw a lot of attention. Consider making your own sign that will have a presence in front of the church. Let your sign tell those passing by that you have something significant going on. Recreate some of the characters from the Bible School material, or make a sign that portrays the theme. The front lawn signs we design are made from three or four full pieces of plywood. Every year we have parents say, "I've been waiting for the sign to go up out front." Find someone who is good with construction, maybe a few retired men, to be responsible for assembling the sign and then erecting it solidly. Consider placing spotlights in front of it to draw attention to the information even when the sun goes down.

Another kind of sign is the yard sign, similar to a real estate or political sign. These can be ordered online and distributed to members of the church who would be willing to put one in their yard. A caution here is to carefully design the sign. Too much information defeats the purpose of someone looking at it. The main information needs to be large enough for someone to read it when driving past. This can be a challenge when you want the sign to include the name of the event, the church name, date, time, and contact information.

Consider making a DVD to distribute. If you have access to the equipment, this could be an excellent promotional tool. Done well, a DVD will send a message that your church strives for excellence and is open to using modern technology. The DVD could include highlights of a similar event that was offered last year. Think about some of the most creative parts of the upcoming event and spotlight them. If puppets will be introduced or a leader in costume will be the emcee, then use them to give out the basic information.

Consider inviting day care centers to make arrangements to transport children to summer activities. The kids in their care rarely get the opportunity to attend day camps, take special lessons, or hang out at the local swimming pool. Provide the centers with flyers and registration forms to send home with each child eligible for your program. Transportation to and from the day care site needs to be addressed thoroughly. Make sure there is sufficient insurance. Also, someone from the day care center needs to stay at the church in case of any problems. You may find that your program interests the day care workers so much that they pitch in to help with activities. In that case, you've not only made contact with a child but also the adult caretaker.

Create community news releases for the local newspaper, radio stations, and television stations. These are free advertising! Before pursuing this form of advertising, consider the size of the community. The most difficult part about community news releases is that they need to be turned in at least three weeks prior to the event. Sometimes, it's easy to get caught up in the mechanics of the event and overlook doing this early on. Community releases should not run over four hundred words and should use short paragraphs of no more than three sentences. Here's a basic structure for constructing a community news release:

1. Put a heading at the top that identifies it as a press release.

2. Identify the newspaper, radio station, or television station it is being sent to, along with the specific person's name in charge of the releases.

3. Identify the organization (church) it is from.

4. Identify yourself and a phone number in order to make contact if they have questions.

5. Indicate today's date and the date of the event.

6. Provide a headline in a concise manner.

7. The first sentence should grab the reader's attention.

8. Immediately supply the basic who, what, when, and where information of the event. Some readers never get any further than this.

9. Briefly tell about the church.

10. Supply a short interesting quote from someone who attended previously.

11. Explain how people can get more information or register.

Ask someone to proofread the final draft to insure you have produced a clean copy. This is a courtesy to the newspaper and will build a good working relationship with them. The less work they have to do to make the release presentable, the quicker it will find its way into print.

Some churches purchase advertising packages from newspapers or radio stations. If a church pays for weekly advertising on the church page, the newspaper will often offer a free center ad several times a year. These do need to be claimed far in advance. Purchasing newspaper ads can be quite costly. My recommendation is that if you are going to run a newspaper ad, insist that it runs anywhere in the paper except the church page. If your church has purchased an annual radio commercial package to use for special occasions, ask if your event could use one of those spots. Commercials are usually one minute in length and need to be timed to within one second before going in to record.

We've found that we get more response from the newspaper when we forego the block ad and use the money to provide a separate insert in the newspaper. The separate piece can be printed anywhere and then given to the newspaper to stuff in the loose ad section. This way of using the newspaper ad draws more attention.

Investigate to see if any large businesses in your town offer a special sign-making service for non-profit organizations. Our local Coca-Cola plant makes large vinyl banners with professional lettering on them free of charge. (Of course, the Coca-Cola logo is displayed on one end.) These can be tied to fences or staked in open lots. Our city street department will hang them over downtown streets if the time period they are to be hung is reserved.

The last form of publicity I want to mention to you is mass mailing. We have found this to be extremely effective, especially if we are using mailing lists of kids with whom we have had previous contact. A mass mailing should make it as easy as possible for the person to become involved in the event. Provide contact and registration information. We usually provide a tear-off form that moms and dads can fill out and mail back to us. More and more, we are finding that parents will register their children by e-mail, so make sure you provide an e-mail contact on your flyer. Once you've created a mail list, send the information out at least three times in different forms. The mailings should resemble one another enough that they are easily identifiable as the same event, but still make the reader want to check it out again.

Publicity is a big job! Recruit someone who has a heart for seeing children come to the Lord to spearhead getting the information out. Consider the budget available to you, and then blanket the targeted area by using as many means of publicity as possible. When people hear and see the information through a variety of methods, it conveys a message. The message is that you're serious about what you're doing and you passionately want children to be part of what's happening.

WELCOMING

One summer, we had 250 kids spread through the building and on the property for Bible School. As I walked the halls, I smiled a lot and paused to acknowledge as many as I could. "McKenzie, did that tooth fall out, yet?" "How high did you build your tower, Colton?" "Don't you have a great leader, Bailey?" Little did I know that I was being watched. The little boy who was spying found the perfect opportunity to confront me. "Do you know *my* name?" he said with his hand over his name tag. "If I'm not mistaken, you're Nick," I answered. You would've thought he had seen the most amazing magic trick. I simply knew his name. It seemed like Nick always made his way toward me when I was engaged in those one-on-one moments. "Hi, Nick, how's your day going?" "Oh, hi Nick, nice job on the ship you built. I saw it drying on the table." "Is that you walking behind me, Nick?"

Then, on the last afternoon, he traced each step I made down the hall, watching as I greeted the kids. "Pastor Tina, you know everybody's name. How come you know everybody's name?" Nick could be difficult and I'm not sure he heard his name spoken very often in a tone that was anything but stern. His words brought me to a halt, though, when I realized the impact my greetings had made on him. "Because God made you special, Nick, and your name is important to Him. Because it's important to Him, it's important to me." I am convinced that the main thing Nick remembers about his first experience at Bible School was that it was a place where they knew his name and it was said lovingly.

That's not an easy task, knowing everybody's name. Maybe you have some secret method of remembering names or are just gifted with putting names and faces together, but for me, it's just down right hard work. And, about the time you think you've got it down, they grow five inches, lose all their front teeth, get glasses, or do all three! There are a few things that you can do that will help you memorize:

❀ Name tags. And don't let the kids fill them out. Write their first name in great big block letters with a fat black marker, so you can see it twenty feet away. If you have to have name tags every time the kids get together, then keep making them.

❀ Talk often with teachers and group leaders about the kids in their care. Connect the children with personal characteristics and friendships they have. The more you talk about the children, the more reference points you develop to go to when trying to remember their names.

❀ If it's a program where there will be lots of children from outside your normal care, handle the registrations and mail lists as much as possible. See the names, even if you haven't met the kids yet. This past year I turned all the Bible School registration and group organization over to people on my team. Normally, I would have known the kids before they even stepped on the property and been able to tell you who invited them, but I was at a loss. I hadn't managed the names in any way. Lesson learned. I'll put myself back in that loop some way this year.

For new kids and their families, the church is a very strange environment. It's a big personal risk to go to a place full of strangers and unfamiliar rooms. Remember your first day of junior high? Remember how frightening the long hallways were? You didn't understand the schedule, and where did they hide the bathrooms? Kids who have been raised in the church think of it as a second home and even know some great hiding places. But for those kids who walk into a church for the first time, there are some things that we can do to help them feel welcome:

❀ Identify leaders and teachers. Give all the workers something to wear that tells new friends, "You can ask me! I'll be able to help you!" It can be a big button, ball cap, t-shirt, or an apron. When we did our circus themed Bible School, we identified all the workers with red and white striped vests. The important thing is that they should all be the same. Even if they can't read, kids will pick up on the fact that they see lots of people wearing the same thing, so they must all be doing the same thing.

❀ Set out landmarks (for those times when you can't personally escort). If a child asks you where he is supposed to go, instead of saying, "Go to the third door on the left," say, "See where the treasure chest is sitting in the hall? Go in that room."

❀ Introduce both the child and their parents to the child's group or class leader. When the child sees that mom or dad has met their leader and the parents apparently think he's safe with them, then the group becomes a safe place to be. The following is also an extremely important part of welcoming parents. While the child is listening, review with the parents where they are to meet their child and at what time. Again, this is part of welcoming both the child and the parent.

Prajin came with his friend, Blake, to the children's activities. The little boy from India enjoyed being with his friend and in the middle of whatever we were doing. It was a rare occasion that I met either of his parents, but on one particular night his mother came to pick up the boys. She waited patiently to speak with me. In her broken English she said, "I want you to know that Prajin tells everyone about the happy place he gets to go." A little boy who got his first exposure to the church where the one true God was worshiped, had made his evaluation. He had decided that it was a happy place to be. He was welcome.

PROVIDE RESOURCES

For almost four years we lived in Pasadena, California, home of the extravagant Rose Parade. In the midst of the parade's beauty, there was almost always a strange story that would surface about something that happened as the flowers were being glued or about the floats as they made their way along the route. Each year, stories of past mishaps and incidents were told once again. My favorite, though, was probably the story of the year that a magnificent float, covered in its blanket of flowers, slowed to a stop midway through the route. The machinery that was powering the float had run out of gas. Even more embarrassing than holding up the parade while someone retrieved gasoline was the fact that the sign on the side of the float showed the sponsor to be Standard Oil Company. One of the largest oil companies in the world, but they failed to tap into the resources that were at their disposal. They had overlooked the small things that would make a big impact. In the same way, there are small resources available to you that will help you make a big impact on kids as you reach them for Jesus.

A few years ago I attended a conference that focused on getting men involved in children's ministry, and even more important, once they got involved, how to keep them there. Over two hundred people were present, mostly women, but also a handful of men who were willing to express themselves. When asked what these men wanted in order to feel supported, they unanimously responded that they wanted to know what was expected of them and they wanted the tools to get the job done. Go stand in the garage or the workshop where a man tinkers with automobiles or carpentry. It's a buffet of gadgets, parts, and tools. Lots and lots of tools. You want to really frustrate a man? Ask him to do a job that he doesn't have the tools for.

If volunteers, men or women, are willing to commit time and energy to children's ministry, then at least offer them compensation by providing the tools they need to accomplish the task. As I present workshops, I ask volunteers who have left a position why they did so. Time and time again I hear it was because they were frustrated by not having the resources they needed. "I come in on Sunday morning, and not even the basics, like construction paper and glue, are provided."

So, what should you provide? You need to come up with a system that works for your church. We like to have basics (like glue, paper, scissors, tape, crayons, markers, pencils) in a small cabinet in each room. But you will have to decide what the basics are for your church. Think through what supplies are going to be needed and make a list. Then, put the list on the inside of the cabinet door. This way, the teacher knows what should be in the cabinet, and if inventory is running low or an item is missing, they know they should contact someone to get it replenished. If they're not sure what's actually supposed to be in the cabinet, then they don't know they should request it. If your rooms are used by other groups throughout the week, then you may need to lock the cabinet, so teachers can count on the supplies they left last week to still be in the cabinet this week.

Then, the really fun part of resources comes when you create a space for items that go beyond the basics. Take any kind of space you can get: a walk-in closet, a classroom that's not in use, or an office that has become a catch-all. Claim it as your "resource room." The resource room is where things to enhance learning experiences are kept in an organized fashion. Special art supplies, such as glitter, colored paper plates, paints, potato chip cans, beads, packing peanuts, yarn, paper sacks, toilet tissue rolls, and wiggle eyes are kept here. Each time you purchase special supplies for a project, you will probably have leftovers. Keeping leftovers without labeling them correctly is just collecting clutter. Keeping leftovers so they can easily be found turns them into future resources. What wasn't enough for a big project may be just right for a teacher who only has three children. The resource room is also where objects to be used in games are kept. These include such things as balls, dice, hula hoops, buckets, bean bags, and plastic bowling pins. Things that can't be gathered in a day should be kept in the resource room so a larger number of them can be accumulated over time.

Keeping storage containers uniform helps to use every inch of your space. Avoid using round containers, because you lose four corners of valuable storage space. Shoeboxes are free, they're easy to open and close, they have a wonderful flat area to use for labeling, and they're strong enough to stack. If you'd rather use plastic, dollar stores usually have plastic shoeboxes for a dollar per box. For little objects, we like to use the metal cappuccino canisters. We usually paint them with bright craft paint so the busyness of the label is covered. Keep your eyes open for interesting containers that people discard. One day in December the church business administrator was preparing offering envelopes for the new year. Six boxes of envelopes were packed in their own cardboard box, a little smaller than a shoebox. My eyes lit up! I scavenged over twenty identical boxes that were perfect for our resource room. Another good container that might be right under your nose at the church is a greeting card box. If you have cards available for the congregation to use, claim the boxes for children's ministry. Budgets are tight for many churches, so use and reuse what you can.

There are two other components of your resource room that are very helpful. Once you've got things labeled, compile an inventory. Distribute copies of this to your workers so they know what is available to them. As things change, update the inventory. The other helpful element to your resource room is identifying someone who will take on the responsibility of keeping items stocked, distributed, and organized. This doesn't have to be someone who has the desire to work with children, but someone who enjoys being behind the scenes and doing meticulous work. Look for someone who has the gift of organization. What seems like a chore or the dirty work may be the ministry that someone else has been searching for.

We've talked about resources that can be put in a cabinet or stored in a room, but let's not overlook the human resource. Sometimes what you need is help in running errands to gather the supplies. There are costumes to be made and a seamstress is needed. Who's going to build that log cabin for Bible School or paint the walls in the preschool room? These people may not prepare lessons or sit on the floor with kids, but they can spur your children's ministry to a new level you hadn't thought possible if you tap into these vital resources.

Broaden the scope of volunteers in children's ministry to involve more than teachers and helpers. When people invest their time, energy, and finances in any organization, they become ambassadors for that organization. There is a sincere desire within most of us to invest in opportunities that have significance and through which an impact can be made. All of us "want to make a difference" in some way.

Look for people who are doing something well and enjoy doing it. Think about how their talent could be put to use in children's ministry. For example: creating fun environments to go along with a special theme generates excitement in the kids. Keep your eyes open for someone who goes all out for their child's birthday party or has helped with the local community theatre. When you draw someone new into the ministry their ideas and experience come with them. Allow yourself to be blown away by what someone else can envision. Someone who likes to tinker with electronics can put together some eye-popping special effects that will mesmerize the kids. Women who have a talent for sewing and can create things without a pattern are invaluable assets. When we were writing an Old West themed Bible School, we came up with a game that needed ten stick ponies. Maxine took some old mop handles and created the most adorable stuffed pony heads to put on them. They've lasted for years and we've used them for all kinds of fun activities. Maxine recently joined Jesus in heaven, but at her funeral the pastor showed one of the ponies that she had blessed the children with. Men who love to work with a scroll saw can make outstanding crafts from thin sheets of wood. It gives these people immense pleasure to be able to use the gifts God gave them to assist in reaching kids for His kingdom.

In addition to talents, keep spiritual gifts in mind. When we think of the gift of hospitality, we tend to think of welcoming newcomers and opening our homes for adult studies. But children need to experience hospitality too. Church needs to be a place where kids are celebrated, not only in big ways, but also in small ways like having a special adult who greets them. Daryl was a retired man who always had his pockets full of Tootsie Rolls. Little and big kids hunted him down every Sunday morning to get their Tootsie Roll. Daryl had the gift of hospitality and he used it in children's ministry, even though he never taught a Sunday school class, led a children's choir, or gave a puppet a voice. What other gifts do you recognize in the people in your congregation that could be used in children's ministry?

Announce the supplies you need in the newsletter or bulletin. Even if it seems like garbage to most people, when they can contribute something to the ministry, they have made an investment. We recently made a request for toaster ovens before we went out to purchase them. I had more toaster ovens than I knew what to do with! By donating, people are buying into what children's ministry is all about.

Think of a service project that will involve the entire church. Our children sponsored a backpack drive, where they collected backpacks that were full of school supplies. The packs were delivered to the school administration office to distribute to kids who were starting school without supplies. The entire church participated. The adults felt as though they were contributing to children's ministry, even beyond our own doors, and the kids felt connected to the church at large. As I mentioned earlier, they have also sponsored an ongoing "can-paign" where they collect aluminum cans and the money goes toward the building fund. A large aluminum garbage can with a sign plastered on the side of it sits outside the main children's room, and every week the kids are reminded of what they are part of.

Imagine the most unlikely person in your church becoming involved in children's ministry. Where could they fit in? How could they invest themselves? Pull as many people in as possible. You need a big team!

PARENTS

There are 168 hours in a week and, more than likely, children are participating in a children's ministry program no more than three hours in the week. Many will be participating less than that, and a few will be more, but still, in relation to how many hours they are outside the realms of the structured ministry, they are participating in programs for a very small percentage of time. It is incredibly important that we use every minute of the precious time with these kids, but it is also necessary that we realize that the bulk of spiritual instruction needs to be done by parents. Look at children's ministry as coming alongside parents to reinforce what is taking place in the home. At the same time, keep in mind that some parents totally neglect this part of their child's life and view the church as the sole provider of spiritual leadership.

If there is support for the idea that parents are their child's spiritual teachers, then children's ministry is a partnership with parents. A large part of what takes place should be equipping parents to use the life situations that happen during play time, car rides, visits to grandma's house, sleepovers, and sports practices as teachable moments for Christ-like living. Programs can talk about how a child should respond in certain situations, but the parents are actually there to engage the child when the situation occurs.

Parents make great volunteers. More than anyone, they want to see children's ministry be successful, because that means their child is getting something of value. They are aware of age development and easily adapt activities to be more age-appropriate. They know what frustrates particular age children and what excites them, because they live with these dynamics every day. As you train parents to lead children in ministry, they learn bundles that carry over into the home. I give each one of my new recruits an *Egermeier's Bible Story Book*, because it retells most of the Bible stories in a biblically accurate way. We also use this same book in an adult study group for people who are just getting acquainted with the Bible. It gives me goose bumps, butterflies, and tingly sensations when I witness the confidence a parent gains in the home by using this resource and leading children in organized activities. Don't think that you're only teaching children.

Work with the senior pastor or teachers of adults to incorporate parenting classes. There is a large assortment of Christian parenting DVDs or guest speakers who lead this kind of training full-time. Many churches use this as an outreach event, because most young parents want as much help as they can get in raising their children. Include equipping parents as part of the children's ministry.

There are a few things to keep in mind that will help parents and children to connect following a children's ministry program. Any craft they take home should have something on it that identifies how it related to a story. We use mailing labels for many of our crafts. If the child has made a big fish by stuffing and painting a brown lunch bag, the child will attach a label that reads: "Jonah was swallowed by a big fish when he ran away from God (Jonah 1:17)." Include the Scripture reference so parents can easily find it if they want to. Let's admit it, sometimes our children's crafts need a little help to identify what they are. These simple labels provide a conversation starter for the parents. Without insulting the child by asking what the craft actually is, the label prompts the parent to explore what the child learned. Now isn't that much more interesting than a fill-in-the-blank take home paper?

One of the major decisions that need to be made about children's ministry is considering how much the family will be involved. Many churches are opting to focus on family ministry where everyone is involved together, children and adults. It's not necessary that the time be totally family or totally children; it can be a mixture of both. Plan special events on a regular basis where the entire family participates together, no matter what the age span.

Both the children's ministry workers and parents want the same thing for children: they want their kids to grow up to be both believers and followers of Jesus Christ. We're on the same team with the same goal, so welcome parents and include them in the children's ministry vision.

CELEBRATE EVERYTHING

Look around. People are celebrating all the time, and many times they don't even know why. When St. Patrick's Day rolls around, you see banks decorating in green, classrooms having special parties, bars tinting their drinks green, and you'd better watch out for a pinch if you're not donning your green apparel. Ask those same people why they're celebrating and my guess is most of them can't tell you who St. Patrick was. The church of Jesus Christ has cause to celebrate—nonstop! We have a responsibility to celebrate when we see God's hand at work in His people, and because one purpose of the church is to grow together in fellowship with one another, we have a responsibility to celebrate the high points in one another's lives.

Whether it's a small milestone of growing up, such as riding a bicycle without training wheels, or presenting a musical that the kids have been pouring themselves into for months, don't let the opportunity to celebrate pass you by. Too many leaders get to the end of whatever they're working on and are just relieved that it's over. Celebration shouldn't be an afterthought but something you have in mind from the onset. Think of celebration as a time when you acknowledge the actual accomplishment, reward the hard work, or recognize progress or changes. It doesn't mean giving a blow-out party each time, but it means finding a way to show respect for the accomplishment. It means including others in the rejoicing, or simply stopping everything for a moment to offer praise. I challenge you to listen to the conversations you have on any one day with an ear to recognizing reasons to celebrate. My guess is you'll hear about birthdays, a successful hit at the Little League game, a scripture that was completely memorized, a friend finally agreeing to come to a church event, that last craft kit being put together for VBS, a child getting an excellent progress report from a tutor, or the secretary putting together a beautiful advertisement. Write them down as you hear them, and you'll be amazed that there are opportunities to celebrate all day long.

What does celebrating do for you as the celebrator, rather than the celebrated? Let's get very selfish here. What's in it for you? Each time you celebrate with someone, you remove yourself for a moment from the stress of what you're dealing with. It raises you to be able to lift others. It reminds you that there is an end, and there will also be cause to celebrate what you're working on. People like to see celebration going on; it's a positive thing and they are drawn to it. When every accomplishment is seen as a cause for celebration, people want to get involved. More than that, though, celebration provides a way to bond with people. The fact that your kids want to share the little successes of their lives is a compliment you should treasure. How many times have you heard a child's voice cry out in excitement as little feet thumped down the hall and stopped in front of you to display a huge smile with front teeth recently gone missing? There's no accomplishment there, except for maybe a little yank or two. But, it's an important time to recognize that a child is growing up. In that moment, you don't have to set helium balloons loose or serve delightfully decorated cupcakes, but what you do need to do is create a moment of celebration. Undivided attention, a few probing questions of what took place to show your interest in the event, topped off with a hug of congratulations. The child walks away with yet another reason to smile that toothless grin: their children's pastor took time to celebrate something important in their life.

Let's look at some ways you can spotlight and celebrate individual kids.

✿ Create a bulletin board where newspaper clippings can be posted. You might not always catch the pictures as they appear in the paper, but periodically write an article for the church newsletter or announce to the children that if they get their picture in the paper you would like to have a copy. Sometimes the articles are difficult to read or the child's name is hidden in the text, so next to the posted clipping make a colorful card that says something like "Maria's team made the city tournament" or "Here's Travis doing what he does best!" Leave the pictures up for at least a month.

✿ On that same bulletin board provide a place where kids or parents can post news about what they're involved in. It may be an upcoming event and the news release might read, "BreAnna's artwork will be on display in the mall March 11–18. Stop by and take a look." Or "Austin's Lego League team got world championship designation at the international competition last week in Atlanta, Georgia."

✿ Recruit one of the older adult Sunday school classes or an individual, who will make it their ministry to watch the newsboard. Ask them to commit to supporting these children by celebrating with them. An unexpected postcard of congratulations does amazing things. One lady decided that she would ask the fast food restaurants for coupons for free ice-cream cones and French fries, which she included in each of the notes she wrote.

✿ Recognize birthdays. It never ceases to amaze me how important birthdays are to children. I would rather get mine over with without anyone noticing, but the cameras can't be pointed in a child's direction long enough when it's their birthday. The most difficult part of sending birthday cards is in the organization and planning. Decide who you're going to send cards to. Will it be all the kids on your mailing list, some of which may only come once a year? Or will you send cards to only those kids who regularly attend?

❧ Many churches give out Bibles as children enter a certain grade or class. Rather than casually passing them out as the kids leave the classroom, make it more of a celebration. After all, this is a time to recognize that they are old enough to take spiritual matters seriously. Invite parents to come to a tea or a "Muffins and Me" breakfast on the week the Bibles are to be passed out. Make it a ten- to fifteen-minute celebration where you stress the importance of using the Bible and declare your pleasure with the children. Take time to write an individual note in the front of the Bible that will become a keepsake for years to come. In this note, share the thoughts of your heart with the child and point out the potential you see in them. Fill out the presentation page so the children can see their names and be reminded of the special time when this was given to them. Many times when you purchase Bibles at Christian bookstores they will emboss the name on the cover for free. How special is that! Only grown-ups usually have their names embossed on their Bibles. And, lastly, take the time to wrap the Bible, even though the child knows what's inside. There's a message sent when you present someone with a beautifully wrapped gift.

❧ If your church has its own Web site, create a celebration page. This could include celebration moments for anyone in the congregation and will be much like the bulletin board, only it's on the Web site. This can be a lot of fun as graphics are added to embellish each article, along with crazy fonts that will draw attention to it. An added benefit of posting celebrations here is that people will log onto the church Web site to see the celebration page and take in the other information while they are there. Caution: check your church policy about postings on the Web site, and never place pictures of children on the Web site without the specific consent of the parents.

In addition to personal celebrations, your children's ministry program should include a celebration each time a group of children are involved, like when a presentation is over (such as a musical), when a series of classes or a study has been completed (such as an eight-week discipleship program), when there is a significant restructuring change or graduation, or when a seasonal program has finished (such as a fall midweek program for preschoolers). There are all kinds of ways to celebrate completion of programs rather than celebrating individuals, so let's look at a few of these ideas.

❀ Celebrate when a presentation has been given. Twice a year our children's choir, Joyful Noise, presents a full-length musical during the Sunday morning worship services. The children prepare for three to five months for these, depending on the season of the year. Near the end of the schedule of rehearsals, after a particularly outstanding practice, we give the children a pizza party to simply say we noticed how hard they were working. We celebrate the children leaving Joyful Noise to move into the youth group by recognizing them at the spring performance. Also, recognized with a token gift at each performance are all the children who had perfect attendance at the rehearsals for that musical. We publicly point out their dedication and commitment to the choir. It's amazing how that little moment of celebration spurs the others' attendance in the next season. They want to be recognized for being dedicated. And, then the parents and staff usually put together a goodie-bag for all the kids to receive after the final presentation. The unique thing about these goodie bags is that the contents are related to the main themes of the musical and Scriptures they are based on. Each item has a card attached that points out that connection—one last attempt to reinforce the message behind the musical.

✿ Celebrate when a series of classes or a study has been completed. Our children's ministry program includes quite a few six- to eight-week topic and age-appropriate programs that the kids sign up for. These programs usually get lots of parental support, so we like to include the entire family in our celebrations. Periodically, we offer a program to our older elementary kids called *Godcalling@yourheart.com* (published by Warner Press). This is a discipleship program that focuses on discovering God's plan for your life. It's serious business and it calls for a great deal of commitment in attendance and completing outside assignments while developing personal faith plans. For our celebration at the completion of this program, we recognize the children in morning worship time and then reserve the back room of the pizza restaurant just a few doors down from the church for lunch that day. The families have been sent an invitation to attend and have been encouraged to contribute to the celebration by doing something special for their child or giving them something that will commemorate this achievement. When witnessing the extent of the celebration, the younger siblings look forward to the day when they will be able to participate in the program.

A similar example is when our six-week study of servanthood called "Unwrapped" concluded. Each child asked a significant adult to join them in the last service project, cleaning out the church storage barn, and then invited them to lunch at the fast food taco restaurant next door. The important significance of this celebration was that children did not necessarily choose a parent to join them. Some kids may want to include a grandparent, a neighbor, a coach, or a scout leader in their celebration.

✿ Celebrate rites of passage. These are times when kids are old enough to move into a new class or into the youth group. One of our Sunday school teachers always has an Aloha Day on the Sunday when kids move up to their next grade level class. Aloha is a generic Hawaiian greeting that means both "hello" and "goodbye." Because her class encompasses two grade levels, only some of the children leave. She decorates her room with an island theme, and then as the children who are graduating leave, the ones who are staying create a path for them to walk through to the door. They place leis around the necks of the departing children and bid them "Aloha." As the new students arrive, they receive the same treatment. A lei is placed around their necks and they are bid "Aloha" as they come through the door. No gifts are exchanged but there's definitely a celebration.

✿ Celebrate when a seasonal program has concluded. Instead of spending our time preparing a closing program for our two separate weeks of Bible School, we have decided that we want to create a family time where people can mingle and feel comfortable on our church site. We want our visitors to know that we consider family a high priority and that we want to develop a relationship with them. Our Bible School is in the morning, so the evening of the last day of VBS we invite everyone back, along with their guests, for a free hot dog dinner. We get children and adults together in the sanctuary where the children sit with their parents as we go through a day's typical opening exercises. Some of our special guests who have been there during the week join us briefly, the children get their parents involved in some of the songs, and introductions of staff are made. We're done in about twenty minutes. We've conveyed the focus of our week and given the guests a glimpse of our enthusiasm for being part of their children's lives. While that is taking place, the kitchen crew is frantically getting dinner ready, free to all our guests. Some of the games the children have played that week are set up outside and we encourage the parents to play along with their child to get the Bible School experience. We bring out the sno-cone machine, spin some cotton candy, pop the popcorn, and have a great time. The added benefit we've found is that out of gratitude the parents stick around to not only clean up, but also to help us get all the decorations down and the supplies put away. Before we leave that night, you would never know there had been a wild and crazy week of Bible School going on.

We've been talking about celebrating a program coming to a close, but what if we made the celebration a learning experience? Did you know that there is a National Pretzel Day? This past spring it was on Wednesday, April 26. Wouldn't it be fun to make a big deal out of celebrating National Pretzel Day, creating all kinds of learning activities using pretzels? The pretzel was created as a symbol of prayer, because hundreds of years ago, instead of putting their hands together when they prayed, they crossed their arms. The pretzel reminded the people at that time of the crossed arms of prayer. There are lots of ideas using pretzels as an ingredient, which can turn snack time into a learning activity. Let kids form human pretzels and then try to get undone without disconnecting. Use this activity to talk about how we are connected in the body of Christ. Check out www.commonconnections.com and www.thevirtualvine.com for ideas on crazy days of celebration you could base your next event on. (Let me warn you, though, some of these ideas are on the silly side, but hey, kids love to be silly!)

Let's not forget the celebrating that needs to happen within the children's ministry team. With your team, celebration in large part is to show appreciation, so take every opportunity to express your gratitude for their faithfulness. When they've shown initiative and created a new activity to go along with a lesson, praise them abundantly and point it out to others. Poke your head into a class and tell the kids what a wonderful teacher they have, encouraging the kids to give a loud whoop and holler for their teacher followed by high fives. Surprise a teacher with a little gift that goes along with the name of their class. Our kindergarten class is called "The Bee-lievers" and uses little bees everywhere. I found two soft, cuddly stuffed yellow and black bees at a discount department store one day. To show my excitement for how they were developing the theme of their class I gave both the teachers one of these bees. One of the teachers has the little bee sitting on the dashboard of her van as a reminder of the Bee-lievers she's committed herself to.

I also like to celebrate when my team comes up with ideas. When I know instinctively that it's a good idea and that the kids are going to respond, my body sends me signals. I get goose bumps from fingertip to fingertip and from the top of my head to the soles of my feet. When someone throws out one of these incredible ideas, we'll look at each other, squeal, and then we start this little chant as if we were going through a checklist.

I say "Goose bumps," and they call out, "Check."

I say "Butterflies," and they respond, "Check."

And then I say "Tingling sensations," to which they respond one final time, "Check."

It's our team's way of interrupting whatever we're doing to celebrate. The benefits are tremendous as it increases our momentum and unifies our team.

Sometimes the celebration has a hidden message. Brother and sister, Jimmy and Lindsay, were kids I had the privilege of teaching. When Jimmy was in elementary school and Lindsay was still a preschooler they were walking along the shore of a lake during a family outing. The two children spotted a fish covered in mud flopping about just out of reach of the water. Jimmy reached down, picked up the fish, washed the mud off of him, and threw him back in the lake. He then turned to his little sister and told her that Jesus did that with people. "Even when people think there's no hope for them, Jesus washes off their sins like the mud covering the fish. When the fish was clean he got thrown back into the lake to live and when Jesus cleans us He sends us back into life to live for Him." I took great pleasure in celebrating how Jimmy had saved the life of the fish, but my personal celebration was that Jimmy had connected the dots. He got it! May you find ways to celebrate when your kids share their little adventures.

CREATIVITY

"If everybody is thinking alike, then somebody isn't thinking."
—General George S. Patton

Creativity: it's going to set you apart. It's going to charge your ministry and it's going to motivate your team. That doesn't mean starting from scratch on every idea and writing all your own lessons, but it does mean giving each thing you do a special twist that leaves your mark, adding just a little more sparkle or pizzazz.

Warning! Warning! Creativity should come with a warning label:

It can be addictive.
It can make more work for you.
It will raise the energy level in your workers.
Children may experience a heightened sense of enthusiasm.
It is highly contagious!

Some of you want to crawl in a hole right now or skip this topic altogether, because you're convinced you're not and never will be creative. Let me make just one small point here and then we'll see if you decide to read on. Isaiah 40:28 names God as "the everlasting God, the Creator of the ends of the earth" (NIV). And then, turn to Genesis 1:26 and read that "God said, 'Let us make man in our image, according to our likeness" (NIV). You don't get to pick and choose which characteristics of God you take on. Isn't that mind-boggling? You and I were created in the image of God to have the characteristics of God. God. The One with the ultimate imagination. God. The Creator, Inventor, Maker. The Endless Source of creativity. Surely He didn't leave us depleted of those qualities. They may be buried, though, because someone has convinced you that your ideas, the way you look at things, don't quite fit the parameters of acceptable creativity. Your ideas may not be the earth-shaking ones that draw a resounding amazement from the crowds, but you do have ideas.

Be encouraged that God imagined you and breathed into you the breath of life—His breath. He gave you an imagination and He wants to help you explore it and use it for His kingdom. There is a story told about a young mother who wanted to expose her son to the beauty of fine music by taking him to a Paderewski concert. Mother and son found their seats, but mother soon saw a friend and went to visit with her for a moment. While she was away the little boy got up to explore the auditorium and found himself behind the large curtain on the stage. The lights dimmed to signal the beginning of the concert and the mother returned to her reserved place to find her son's seat empty. Then, she heard the simple notes of "Twinkle, Twinkle, Little Star." There on the stage at the beautiful grand piano was her little boy, pecking out the notes to the only song he knew. Paderewski came out on stage to find the little boy in his place at the piano. A heart of encouragement and a moment of great creativity overcame the renowned pianist as he sat down next to the little one who continued to play. "Twinkle, Twinkle, Little Star" never sounded so grand as it did when Paderewski reached around one side of the boy to add a bass part with his left hand and a running obligato with his right. A simple frightening and embarrassing situation transformed because one man let loose his creativity. God wants to do the same thing. He wants to wrap His arms around us and assure us that He will add great creativity to our simple investment of what we already know.

The more I learn about joy, the more I'm able to incorporate it into my life. When I experience servanthood and learn the possibilities of serving others, I'm able to incorporate it into my daily patterns. It's the same for creativity. Learn about it. Find out what develops it and what releases it in you. Every thought you have is a creative thought. The question is not whether you are creative or not. The question is whether or not you make yourself aware of how you can exercise, develop, tap into, and purposefully use the creativity God has put in you. Now are you with me?

A quick look at the science of the brain and also the science of creativity will help us understand more. The brain avoids atrophy by creating new neural pathways. (There's those fascinating pathways again!) These pathways are a way of exercising the brain and keeping it flexible and strong. They occur when you experience new thoughts or try to solve new problems. Most of us fail to challenge our brains, because we settle for thinking about our daily lives in the same way, day in and day out. Consequently, this habitual type of thinking causes the brain to lose its flexibility, hence, its creativity. Thankfully, there are actions we can take to help open those neural pathways, which we're going to talk about later in this section. Let me bore you just a little more with the science of the brain. Most everyone has a dominant side to their brain—right or left. People who regularaly challenge both the left and the right side of their brains are the people who are usually considered more creative. Although they have a dominant side, the difference between the strengths is slight. What we gather from this is that cooperation between the sides of the brain and an evenness in their strength improves creativity. For those people who primarily use one side of their brains, there are exercises that can be done to strengthen the cooperation between the two sides of the brain. If this is so, then it must be that we can also strengthen our ability to be creative. There are a few rather simple ways to decrease the dominance of one side of the brain, even though they may seem a little quirky and trivial. Regularly working puzzles of all kinds is one way. And another is to physically exercise where you use one side of the body and then do the same action with the other side of the body, such as walking or lifting hand weights one at a time. In addition to strengthening the relationship between the right brain and the left brain, there are some triggers you can employ that will facilitate the release of your creativity.

Humor

Did you know there is a scientific basis for Proverbs 17:22 where it says that "a cheerful heart is good medicine"? Laughing stimulates the release of endorphins, which cause a sense of well-being. After a good laugh, the body is much more relaxed. When the brain is relaxed, then it is more flexible and more accepting of new information. Laughter allows you a moment of detachment from your present situations (possibly stressful ones), and, in that moment, there is a window of creativity. I once heard someone speaking about the effectiveness of good presentations. They said that a great speaker or presenter will make you laugh three times more than a good speaker or presenter. Laughter relaxes your brain and gives it a greater opportunity to accept new information, while your ability to perceive in creative ways is enhanced. Your desire to reach beyond your present boundaries is stimulated, and that's the essence of a creative attitude. So, if you want to release your creativity, find humor in the little things and laugh more.

Here's one way it works. Let's say you're leading the initial planning meeting for the upcoming Bible School. You're hoping it will be an exciting, creative brainstorming session. Think of some humorous things you can do to relax the participants so that their minds are more flexible. Start off with a humorous video clip about children's ministries or show a video of a funny memory from last year's VBS. Read a funny article. Check out www.kidology.org for some good ones.

In another context, if it is true that humor releases creativity, think about it in terms of children's ministry. When puppets make the children laugh, they're opening up the neural pathways for new information to enter. When a themed character, such as Chef Bakesalot (my pretend food network television host) visits a classroom with an object lesson, the children laugh at some of the antics, but also moan when the crazy personality has to leave. In addition to the visual impact, one of the main reasons skits are so effective is because they interject a moment of comedy. VeggieTales can credit part of its success to the fact that children find the characters funny and then are open to the message the stories convey. Preachers understand now that "lightening up" occasionally in a sermon is a healthy thing because people are willing to listen for longer periods of time when they laugh occasionally.

Inspiration

Another area to look at when you want to release your creativity is the role inspiration plays. Inspiring stories of people who have overcome tremendous odds, who have achieved goals, and who have endured hardships offer encouragement for us to reach a little further. The Bible is full of these kinds of stories, but don't neglect present-day people who have their own inspiring stories. Because of the examples they set, they are granting you permission to reach a little further or to take another step, which, in turn, grants you permission to exercise your own creativity. I have personally dealt with crippling rheumatoid arthritis since my eighteenth birthday, and have endured thirty-nine surgeries and a myriad of treatments. Apparently, my story inspires the people around me. I don't intend it to be that way; it just happens. I can't tell you the number of times, though, that people have come to me and said, "I was in so much pain last night and then I thought of what you go through all the time. It made me stop and try to figure out how to cope with the pain, get around it, and keep going." In other words, my story inspired them to be creative with how they dealt with their own situation. Inspiration releases creativity.

Let's go back to the Bible School planning meeting we mentioned a little bit ago. How can you use inspiration to get the creative juices flowing? Recall a touching moment from last year's Bible School. Maybe someone in your church came to know the Lord because of a decision that was made at VBS years ago. Ask that person to briefly share their story so that the participants at your meeting see the urgency and the importance of what they are doing. It will inspire them to let down the walls that have held their creativity captive.

Find a Creative Environment

The next thing you want to do is to find your atmosphere or environment of creativity. This is the place where you feel most comfortable to think and dream. Maybe it's not a particular place, but rather the objects you choose to put around you that focus your thoughts. Some people find they become a fountain of ideas when they are in a group setting, feeding off others in the room. Personally, that is very difficult for me unless I have an established relationship with everyone in the room and I feel safe letting my ideas out. Once a year I go to a writers' conference where I spend a week with my curriculum writing team. The team is usually made up of one writer I have a relationship with from previous years, but the rest of the team are new writers I've never met until that week. It is one of the most difficult environments for me to be creative in, because I don't know the people I'm working with. I can take the same assignment to my "writing hole" at home where I have my resources, where I'm comfortable (my chair is cushy), where I can have absolute quiet and shut the window shades. There I can get a lesson put together quickly, with ease, and it's exciting for me. That's what I've discovered about how I release my creativity. You may need music playing, bright sunshine coming through the window, and to be sitting on the floor. Or you may be able to let loose anywhere as long as you have inspirational objects around you.

Another thing I've learned is that my creativity does not flow on demand, and this has a lot to do with finding that environment. People will call me and ask for an idea of what to do with a lesson they're going to be teaching in an hour, assuming that I can spit it out right then and there. It's not my environment and I clam up and go brain-dead. You will find that some environments, some people, some situations, threaten your creativity. So, when you need to call on those creative juices, don't fight it. Just put yourself in the environment that provides the atmosphere where you feel most comfortable. However it happens, the goal is to gather the best ideas you (personally or with a group) are able to produce.

Let's return once again to that Bible School planning meeting. Create an environment that speaks to the theme you have chosen for the VBS. You're probably already planning to do that for the actual Bible School, but do it for the meeting also. If you're using a construction theme, then serve ice cream in little hard hats, dress as a construction worker to run the meeting, put toy dump trucks on the tables filled with candy, and drape yellow caution tape around the room. Visually, you now have a creative environment for coming up with ideas.

Open Your Eyes

Look around! What great ideas do you see in action around you? How do you process that idea when you see it? Do you say, "Oh, isn't that a neat thing to do"? Or do you write down what you've seen and what ideas it sparks, so it can be tucked away for inspiration at another time? Digest someone else's idea and use it as inspiration to go a different direction to meet the needs of your particular ministry. It's laughable to look back after a program is over and see the little idea that sparked the whole thing.

File, file, file! You will be so thankful you took the time to discipline yourself with filing. Organize articles and ideas you've clipped from magazines, so you can go right to them when you're looking for something on that topic. It's a time-consuming job, but there's never a day that goes past that I'm not glad I made myself do it. Recently, one of the retired ladies at church has volunteered to keep the articles I pull from magazines filed for me. All I do is mark the name of the file on the top of the article and stick it in a folder at the end of my desk. She checks the folder regularly and puts everything in its place. It's one more way someone can invest in children's ministry. (Did you know there are filing angels?)

Look at common objects and see how many uses you can come up with. Hold it a different way. Pour things through it. Try to catch something in it. This is how we came up with the idea to paint with a flyswatter to make fish net, use bath puffs to sponge paint a rainbow, turn a yogurt drink bottle into a snowman, and put ice cream buckets on our heads to play a game of pitch and catch. Check out your garage, kitchen cabinets, and closets. Or, take a field trip to a garden center, home improvement center, or toy store with the sole intention of looking at the objects there in a different way. (Don't forget, they have surveillance cameras, so save the real craziness for when you get home!)

Surround Yourself

Put yourself in the presence of creative people. It's contagious! They ask themselves questions, whether intentionally or instinctively because they've learned that creativity has channels. In children's ministry you'll see that the people you consider creative will ask themselves questions such as:

❀ How can I bring in the senses to this story so the kids can experience it more fully?

❀ What could I place in the room to create an environment the children would relate to?

❀ What kind of technology could I employ that the kids would identify with?

❀ Who could I bring into this lesson to add variety and different talents?

❀ Who might have the supplies I'm looking for?

❀ What object does this story make me think of?

When you're planning that initial meeting, invite people you feel are in touch with their creative side, people who are comfortable together, people who easily give permission to others to stretch their boundaries, and people with special talents or expertise related to the theme you'll be talking about. This should make for an exciting and contagious time of creative exploration together.

As a children's pastor, you not only have the desire and responsibility to develop your own creativity, but you need to encourage and nurture it in your team. Here are a few things you can do to accomplish that.

❉ Expose your volunteers to other children's ministries so they see what is going on at a church where the ministry to kids is charged and vibrant.

❉ On a regular basis, send your team members an article about a creative idea (with pictures, preferably). Include a note from you that simply says that you thought this was a great idea and it made you think of them.

❉ Model creativity. The example of a Bible School meeting we have been following was a way of modeling creativity by setting up the environment so that the participants' creativity could be released.

❉ Encourage and reward creative ideas. Take pictures of what teachers are doing in their classrooms and send it to the writers of the curriculum. (You've got double duty out of that encouragement, rewarding both the teacher's and the writer's creativity.) Brag on ideas in front of the one who came up with the idea.

❉ Share your ideas and ask for input.

❉ Guard against changing an idea simply because of your personal preference.

❉ When a teacher has an idea they really want to implement, do your very best to supply them with the resources to accomplish it.

❉ Provide opportunities for volunteers to exercise their creativity. In the Bible School meeting with a construction theme, you could form groups of three and give each group a traffic cone. Ask them to come up with as many different uses for it as they can (including all phases of the event, such as advertising, decorating, games, activities, and snacks).

❀ Assure your team members that they are just that—part of a team—and every idea does not have to come from one person.

I'd like to return to one of the items from the above list for just a moment, because this is such an important issue. When a member of your team has an idea, and then musters the courage to come and present it to you, move it to the top of your attention list. Apparently, this is something that time and energy has been put into. Your reaction and subsequent action will speak volumes to the validity you put in that team member's creativity. The idea may take some tweaking or adjusting, but the team member needs to know that you are willing to invest in the idea. Especially if this is the first time the team member has brought an idea to you, it's imperative that you take some action toward making it happen. Even if it never happens, the reason for it will be something outside of your control.

The beauty of utilizing the creativity of many people is that it fosters ownership in the ministry. Once people see one of their ideas in action, it's like part of them has become important to the ministry. People who aren't interested in working with a group of kids can still have creative input, which expands the base of the ministry, because more people are feeling part of it and acquiring ownership.

What one thing in this section stuck out to you as a way you can take a step in releasing your personal creativity? Start now, knowing that a healthy dose of creativity can make your children's ministry more conducive to learning, more inviting and assuring for parents, and more enjoyable for you and your team.

How are you going to use one thought from this section to encourage creativity in your team members? Remember that you will feed off of and inspire one another as you release your creativity. Go, and minister in the image of the Creator God!

TRAINING

For years I heard at workshops and seminars that training was a key to expanding children's ministry. It sounded nice, but training events were expensive and my budget was small. I was struggling to find the time and funds to go myself. And, after all, I was teaching most of the classes and leading most of the events; and did I mention, working day and night to do it? I loved being with the kids and getting that immediate gratification of seeing them light up with understanding. If I trained other people, then I would have to let them take my place in some of those experiences! I worked hard and devoted every ounce of energy and passion I could muster to building a well-rounded program. The ministry grew and the church felt the effects of families being reached. The church was steadily growing by building a base of young families with lots of kids and a wonderful momentum had been created. I discovered something that, up to that point, I really wasn't sure existed: there was a limit to what I could do! Consequently, I made the decision to give this "training leadership" thing a trial period of one year. I would intentionally devote myself to building a team and providing them with the training they needed. I would either prove everybody wrong or find out that training really is essential.

The first thing I did was prepare myself for putting the children's ministry programs in a mode where we weren't going to try to build on anything or expand during this year. We would continue on as we had done last year, but nothing new would be added. I decided that a huge amount of my energy should go into building up the people I already had working in children's ministry. Notice, I didn't call us a team at this point. One of the huge benefits of training is that it is a wonderful team builder. I needed to shepherd these people and encourage them in what they were already doing, rather than giving them a job to do and being thankful it was filled with a warm body.

My first step as I looked into training was to recruit one person to join me in attending the Children's Pastors Conference put together by INCM (International Network of Children's Ministry). I had been to these huge four-day events and, even though I had been in children's ministry for over twenty years at that point, I still came away with so much to think about and try. Heidi, a mother of three children under the age of six, seemed to be my likeliest candidate to persuade to go. She was one of my most devoted workers, had a positive attitude toward children's ministry, and was open to what the Lord wanted for her. Heidi had come to me in tears on several occasions recently because of a terrible work situation she was in. As the time got closer and we made preparations to go, I strongly felt that God was leading Heidi out of her present job and into children's ministry. I also felt that the week at CPC was going to be a turning point for her. I hadn't even given this "training thing" its first chance and I was already having lofty ideas of what was going to come from it. I arranged for us to have separate rooms and gave Heidi a king-size bed that she could have all to herself, free from children and pets. As the time for us to go to Atlanta grew closer, each day I sent her an encouraging e-mail as part of the countdown before we left.

The Children's Pastors Conference did not disappoint me, and Heidi could hardly contain herself with all that she was taking in. Sometimes we would go together to workshops, and other times we would split up and then I'd find a time for her to tell me what she had learned. After the conference was over, we had a couple of hours to wait in the hotel lobby before we took our ride to the airport. With our legs flung over the sides of big overstuffed chairs, I looked at Heidi and said, "Well, what did you think?"

She responded, "I called Brad last night and talked to him about quitting my job when I get home. I'd like to volunteer with you about twenty-five hours a week and follow you around. That is, if you wouldn't mind." Her reply dumbfounded me. Even though I had strongly felt God was leading her in this direction I was still taken aback by the words that actually came out of her mouth.

Wow! I felt like I had hit a home run on the first time up to bat. By giving one person a big picture of what was possible in children's ministry, I had duplicated my energy and impact. She was a recruiting machine for the next year's CPC the moment we returned home. Within five weeks she had quit her job, and she still works at least three full days a week at the church, in addition to Sundays. (If you'd like to find out more about Children's Pastors Conferences hosted by INCM, log on to www.incm.org.)

Honor your volunteers by providing training for them. Volunteers aren't asking to be paid monetarily, but they do look forward to the gratification of doing a good job for the Lord. If you approach training as a way to wrap your arms around your volunteers to encourage them to be all that God wants them to be, then you have given them a wonderful gift. Be careful, though, not to approach training as a way of communicating to your volunteers that, "I don't think you know what you're doing, so I'm going to get you some help." You should always include yourself as a participant in the training events, unless you're actually the one presenting, because it conveys the message that there is never a time when you don't need refreshment, new ideas, and an energy boost.

I have discovered some wonderful benefits to investing in training volunteers. When I'm bringing people onto the team, it's not because I'm replacing someone who has decided to stop. In almost all cases, I'm merely building onto what already exists. When people are equipped, they feel capable of doing what they've been asked to do. You're telling them that you see something within them that is worth investing in; you give them value and confidence.

Another benefit that comes from training is that you have happy volunteers. Happy volunteers interact with children in a more positive manner, which means happy kids. And they form friendships with other teachers who love what they are doing too.

Training volunteers energizes them and provides motivation. Every night I plug in my cell phone to be recharged so I can count on it the next day. Training does the same thing for your volunteers. It charges them up, and when they're excited about what they're doing, they're more dependable. With that occasional boost, you can count on your volunteers to do the job that God has set before them. For someone who is working with children's ministry for the very first time, going to a large training event can be overwhelming. I always encourage my people to come home with one major thing they are going to change or work on. Keep all the other ideas that you gathered in a notebook or in the back of your mind, but stick with that one issue. If they don't focus on that one thing, they'll scatter themselves in too many directions and lessen the likelihood of being successful in any. I still do this for myself. Come away with one gold nugget that is going to make you a better leader.

Training gives new or renewed vision. You may be depleted from working tirelessly at putting together a comprehensive children's ministry and feel like you're not even close to where you should be. Networking with other children's workers at a convention or workshop is a great encouragement and wonderful pool of stories and lessons learned. An option or new approach that someone else has tried could be the answer that you are looking for but haven't thought of. Learn from the mistakes and successes of others, That's training in itself.

Trained volunteers become trainers for new recruits. My veteran teachers understand that one of their main goals as a teacher is to train someone to the point where they can be set free to lead a group of their own with the same competency. When it's time to bring on a helper for a class, a "teacher-in-training," I consult the lead teacher about who we might recruit. Who would they feel comfortable with and in whom do they recognize gifts that could be used in children's ministry? We talk about it, and after input from the team, the lead teacher is usually the one who approaches the recruit. Heidi was one of my lead teachers. We agreed that her friend, Heather, should come on as her assistant. They worked together as though every move had been orchestrated. Step by step, Heidi handed over one activity after another for Heather to lead, and then it came time for her to substitute as lead teacher. Heather's confidence grew. Circumstances changed and we thought a lead teacher of an older class was going to be moving away immediately. We needed someone who understood our team and the way we were using the curriculum to take over the class. I went to Heidi and Heather and presented my solution to the problem we had: the two of them needed to split and take on two more people to train. Oh my, the tears were not pretty! You would've thought they were never going to see one another again. I asked them for other solutions, but even with the thought of separating, they knew that's what needed to be done. They both chose new assistants and are doing a beautiful job training them week in and week out. Heather has taken her teaching skills to a new level; giving her more responsibility has released creativity and innovation within her that amazes all of us. Equipping people creates equippers.

Provide a variety of training opportunities. Let's just buzz through some of the ways you can do that.

❀ *During teacher meetings.* Decide on one topic to cover at a teachers' meeting. Make it something the teachers can put to use the very next time they are with kids so they'll get an opportunity to try out the skills or concepts they learned. Also, at teachers' meetings, give teachers a time to share practical things they have learned. Learn from one another's mistakes and ah-ha moments. Take time to work through the unit that they are entering to demonstrate how a lesson can be planned.

❀ *Attend a national conference,* such as the Children's Pastors Conference (CPC), or those presented by Willow Creek Community Church or Saddleback Church. Registration, lodging, food, and travel expenses can make these expensive, but they are worth every penny. Build some of it into the budget, if possible, and then do fund-raising if you have to in order to go. I can guarantee that attending a CPC will have immediate results. Because CPC is not connected with one specific publisher or church, they present an all-inclusive experience. During every workshop session there are about fifteen different topics of interest covered. If you took someone who was mainly interested in ministering to preschoolers, there is a different workshop at each session to deal with preschoolers. The same goes for music, preteens, nursery, development, and many more. And, the people at INCM have made it nice for you, because you can get on their Web site and see the workshop descriptions before you even leave home. Our team actually sits down and plans out a strategy of what each of us will attend before we leave home, so that we can get as much as possible out of the experience. The people you take will come back like little wind-up toys. Set 'em down and let 'em go!

❁ *Attend a regional workshop.* INCM and Group Publishers conduct these throughout the year in locations all over the country. They are reasonably priced and are usually no longer than five hours.

❁ *Bring in a guest professional.* It's always nice to hear a new voice. A guest has a fresh perspective, can see things as a visitor might see them, and can offer insight. They also don't have relationship issues that they are going to have to deal with later on, so their comments can be unobstructed. Being an outside presenter is one of the things I feel a strong call toward and love to do. Churches host a full day or an entire weekend of children's ministry workshops. The guest (an experienced children's pastor) comes in to offer their expertise, recommendations, and encouragement. These can be personalized to the specific needs of your congregation, and your volunteers get an opportunity to talk one-on-one or in small groups with the presenter.

❁ *Take your volunteers on a retreat.* Include lots of time to relax. Do something silly that tells them how much they are appreciated. Then, intersperse training videos, idea exploration, and goal setting. Retreats have excellent potential to solidify teams.

❁ *One-on-one training.* Bring one person on to mentor. Invest yourself in training one person and you will multiply your effectiveness. Be there when they have questions. Demonstrate teaching methods. Point out development differences. Spend time helping one person see a clear and broad picture of children's ministry.

❁ *Send training DVDs or CDs home.* Offer a library of these and let your volunteers know your expectations. Most people have "dead times" in their day when they don't really want to be on the go or they're caught in the car during the commute to work. These are perfect times to slip a DVD or CD in to supply a charge for ministry.

✿ *Provide* K! Magazine *or* Children's Ministry Magazine *for your volunteers.* These magazines come out every other month and are full of ideas for all age groups. They are also the prime places to find out about new resources that are on the market. (Subscribe for *K! Magazine* at www.kidzmatter.com and *Children's Ministry Magazine* at www.childrensministry.com.)

Many people are at a loss as to how a training meeting should be put together, so let's give you a few guidelines to consider.

✿ *Make your teachers feel special.* Choose a theme for the meeting and decorate according to that. Post encouraging quotes and Scriptures on the walls, table tents, or on placemats. Prepare an appreciation gift that goes along with the theme you have chosen. And don't give into the temptation to ask the teachers to bring something. All you want from them is their time and attention.

✿ *Mail! Mail! Mail!* Send an invitation or notice of the meeting. Include a response card with it that shows some humor. And then, send a reminder card timed so they receive it the day before the meeting. Complete your homework to get everyone there, or it defeats the purpose.

✿ *Be ready when the first person arrives.* Greet your volunteers personally as they arrive, which means that you need to be the first one there. Be completely set up, so you can focus your attention on people. Make any necessary introductions and encourage people to talk with one another. Display a discussion starter question that goes along with the theme.

❀ *Get volunteers to sign in.* You can use a traditional pad, but why not write their names on a giant Post-It note, a balloon, your t-shirt, or a cutout that goes along with your theme.

❀ *Set up the room differently each meeting.* Try to have the right number of chairs, without a lot of extra seats. The room chosen for the meeting should be cozy for whatever size group you have. You can meet at tables, in a circle of chairs, clusters of chairs, rows, or hold your meeting in a different classroom each time. This will give everyone an opportunity to take a closer look at how other rooms are set up.

❀ *Begin on time! Finish on time!* Late stragglers will get the idea that they've missed something (especially if the first thing you do is give out a door prize). Starting on time communicates the message that this is important. Honoring the time commitment you asked people to give also conveys that you recognize their time is precious and appreciate their participation.

❀ *Start with an activity.* Not just any activity, but one that turns everyone's attention to the topic of the day. Encourage everyone to interact, talk, and move.

❀ *Deliver a short devotional that is both inspirational and motivational.* It would be very appropriate at this time to share something that has recently happened in children's ministry that indicated children were "getting it."

❀ *Encourage your teachers to be creative.* Give them something to do where they will have to design, build, write, or put something to music. Again, make sure it stays connected to the theme and topic.

❂ *Briefly review your church's mission statement, and keep it visible.* This grounds the team so they are reminded of how their ministry fits into the big picture.

❂ *Talk about one training topic.* Some topics might be: storytelling techniques, discipline, understanding reading levels, how to ask questions, multiple intelligences, explaining salvation to a child, using puppets, or integrating snacks into the story. If you feel uncomfortable presenting a topic, there are training videos available to use with your volunteers.

❂ *Add a little fun and craziness* with prizes, funny announcements, or photos you've taken.

❂ *Model good teaching* by incorporating several of the multiple intelligences (music smart, self smart, people smart, body smart, picture smart, nature smart, math smart, and word smart).

❂ *Ask for specific questions about classes or things* that are going on in individual classrooms: "What can I do for you?" "Are there supplies you need?" "Do you have a wish list?"

❂ *Follow-up the meeting the next day* with notes or e-mails to those who missed the training and thank you notes to those who attended.

A good resource for topics to cover in these training meetings is *Teacher Training on the Go* by Keith Johnson; this resource will give you a starting place. Decide how often you need a teachers' meeting and then schedule dates for the next year. Keep in mind that one of the main goals of training is to motivate volunteers, so don't leave too much time between them, but refrain from being so anxious that you overdo it.

As a leader, your volunteers need to see that you are searching out training opportunities for yourself. When you return from a workshop or conference, share with them some of the ideas you picked up. Make a little packet of ideas or bring back a new tool or game they will be able to use. Devour *K! Magazine* and *Children's Ministry Magazine.* I spend an entire day going through one magazine, dissecting it, and filing away ideas. Any new product that makes me curious, I investigate online or call the company to find out more. Just like your volunteers, training will stimulate you and infuse you with enthusiasm. Likewise, your volunteers will glean motivation from seeing that you are moving forward personally.

As the Scriptures talk about using the gifts God gave us, Ephesians 4:12 tells us that it is our responsibility to equip God's people to do ministry. It's not just a good idea; it's a responsibility. The leadership of the church is responsible for providing not only the construction paper, markers, and bean bags for teaching, but also the training that builds up the teacher. That's where the real equipping happens!

EVALUATION

In order to improve at anything you must debrief and evaluate. Debriefing is the time spent immediately following an event or class time when you gather all the information about what happened. Every single event or class needs to have its own debriefing time arranged. It doesn't matter how big or how small the event—a week-long Bible School or a one-hour Sunday school class—all need to be debriefed. And what's the purpose of debriefing? It's to make your event better and easier next time, and to strengthen you and your workers, so that you can more effectively meet the needs of children. The improvement may lie in the way the event is advertised, the amount of food purchased, the way registration is set up, the pairing of people to responsibility, or it might be personal changes that act as self-training. But, oh my, how relieved you're going to be next year when you pull out those debriefing notes and have so many ideas for improvement. This is when you'll realize what an invaluable tool debriefing is. You may even have fewer reasons for Tylenol!

If you're new to debriefing, it would probably be wise to get used to it on your own before attempting to facilitate a meeting. Try debriefing smaller events or teaching times to acquaint yourself with the process and the benefits. But, once you have a handle on it, you definitely need to add the feedback of others to get a more well-rounded view. Before entering a meeting, take some time to review your own thoughts and write them down. If the team is having a difficult time getting started, you can use your notes as a springboard. Your notes will also give you time to organize your thoughts pertaining to handling any touchy situations where personalities or feelings may be involved. There may be notes in your personal debriefing that you don't plan to share with the team, because they seem harsh to say out loud, although the note may prove beneficial as you personally prepare next time.

Some people like written evaluations rather than a debriefing pow-wow, because they feel free to say what they think and get it in the right words without hurting any feelings. It also gives them a little extra time to ponder. If you choose to have written evaluations involved in debriefing, you'll need to keep in mind to make the added effort to make sure they get turned in. Personally, I find it easier and actually a time saver to avoid written debriefing statements. Part of the benefit of debriefing is the immediate reaction of what took place and that seems to flow better when it's in person.

Who should you include in the debriefing? The key people who served as leadership at the event should definitely be present, but asking all members of the team who participated would also be beneficial. They provide more sets of eyes and ears that observed from unique perspectives. This would be a wonderful time to carry out the event theme one last time and give each person an appreciation gift for taking time to contribute in the debriefing time.

How do you facilitate a debriefing meeting? The facilitator should begin by sharing statistics, comments, reactions from parents, anything that would be very positive and remind everyone that the event was successful. If a worker has shared with you a positive comment from a parent or something a child said, ask that person to tell the group about it rather than you sharing all the "good stuff." Set down a few guidelines at the beginning, reminding everyone that you are not here to blame anyone or point out personal inadequacies. This is a time when we want to recognize the strengths and make note of the weaknesses, reflecting on every detail and how it impacted the event. Each one of these points reflects not on one person but on the presence of the church in general, and the children's ministry specifically. Create a non-threatening atmosphere where everyone's input is respected and acknowledged. Even when talking about difficulties, try to keep the discussion from getting too heavy. We're here to acknowledge these problems; we'll deal with the actual solutions in depth before the next event. You also want to remind everyone that even though the event was a success this year, you want next year's to run smoother and be even better. I once had a snack worker smear chocolate pudding all over her face and hands and jokingly threaten to hurt me if I ever decided to let 250 preschoolers make mud (pudding) in a ziplock bag again. What she was actually saying, in her own warped way, was that some changes in that activity were necessary. We all laughed, but we got the point, and no one's feelings had been wounded.

That situation could have easily hurt someone's feelings. It is imperative that you guard the conversation and set a positive tone. If a potentially hurtful comment is made, you could lose workers if you're not prepared to circumvent it. In the notes you make before the debriefing begins, you may already have an idea of a rough place that's going to be brought up, so figure out how you're going to handle it before standing before the team.

Provide everyone with pencil and paper, because as the discussion goes, it will trigger other thoughts the participants may have that are not appropriate at that time, but will fit in later. It will keep people from getting sidetracked and from inappropriately bringing up topics. Also, this allows people who are not comfortable with bringing something up publicly the opportunity to give you their thoughts on paper.

Post the order of topics you will cover on the board or give each person a copy of your agenda. One way to approach this is to start debriefing with the first thing you had to do as you prepared (possibly recruiting or publicity) and work your way to the event. Then, start with the first issue as the people arrived (possibly parking or registration). Make sure each thing on the agenda is covered before moving on to the next. Chaos can easily ensue if you don't stick with it, because people will head off on tangents that are way down the list. That's why the paper and pencil are important.

A sample order for debriefing an event, let's say Bible School, might be:

Publicity
Recruiting
Preparations / Decorations
Preregistration
Property accessibility
Registration
Opening time (music, puppets, object lessons)
Discovering passwords
Snack areas

Craft areas

Story reinforcement areas

Game areas

Bible exercise areas

Closing time (passing out trinkets, getting kids to their transportation)

Exiting property

Closing program

The questions should be open-ended, asking for something other than a yes or no, but if the person can respond with a simple yes or no, be sure to ask for an explanation. From open-ended questions you are able to get much more detailed feedback.

In each of the above areas, you want to cover the following questions. Some of these questions are appropriate for some areas and not for others.

✿ What went well?

✿ What needed improvement?

✿ Did we accomplish what we set out to do?

✿ What do you think was the kids' favorite part?

✿ What surprised you as far as the way the kids received it?

Debriefing time should be as soon after the end of the event as possible, while information and reactions are still fresh. Take notes on everything that is said. If the information feels inadequate, feel free to ask people to expand on their comments. Changes to the event can be discussed later, using the information that you gathered. When you're finished asking the set of questions you have prepared for the debriefing, encourage anyone else to ask questions or add on.

For each event, the director or children's pastor, whoever was ultimately in charge of the event, needs to do a personal evaluation. Why? Because it encourages improvement. You need to sit back and experience the entire event in your mind, exposing yourself, and taking note of the feelings each part of it evoked. Even more, though, you need to be brutally honest with yourself. Now, don't get defensive with me. Were there things you insisted on doing that someone else could have taken care of? Were your expectations and directions clear to all of the workers? Were there people you failed to communicate with and assumed they knew what you wanted them to do?

With both the team debriefing and the personal leadership debriefing accomplished, now it's terribly important to type up all that information, making sure every point is expanded upon sufficiently. Don't assume that you can remember all the things that were covered. Tuck the report away in a file where you'll go first thing before starting next year's planning. I like to keep a notebook that contains my debriefing reports for all events, and then I also include a copy as the first thing I see when I open last year's file. That way, I'm sure I'll find it easily.

Do you know when you're going to enjoy debriefing an event the most? Next year! When you get ready to start the planning for an event and pull out the file that has ways for it to run smoother and for the kids to benefit more from it, you're going to want to throw confetti in your office and bring out the kazoos. If you let your debriefing guidelines lead you through the next event, I'm sure you're going to find that each time it gets easier and the number of issues you have to deal with will lessen.

Before leaving the subject of debriefing, let's approach it from one other angle. As the children's pastor, you need to teach your team how to do individual debriefing for the classes or groups they lead. Help them see debriefing as an important personal training tool, urging your teachers to spend a few short minutes after each lesson asking themselves the following questions. These questions are similar to those used for event debriefing, but need to be addressed more personally. I suggest you copy these down and give each teacher their own personal laminated copy to carry in their supply bag or put with their curriculum.

✿ What went well? (Give yourself a high five!)

✿ Was there a time when the kids' attention waivered? (Did I stay with one activity too long? Was there something distracting taking place inside or outside the classroom? Did one of the children arrive with a "special" attitude today? Did I allow a child to hold onto a new toy while the lesson was going on, instead of putting it in a safe place?)

✿ What can I do to prevent that from happening next time?

✿ What part of the lesson could have been better prepared?

✿ Was there anything in the lesson that seemed too advanced or too preliminary for this class?

✿ Was it obvious how each element of the lesson connected to the others? If not, how could I have bridged it better?

✿ Were there supplies that were not available? If so, who should I contact to get those supplies?

✿ What one thing will I do to improve next week's lesson?

If you start a debriefing ritual each week, I can tell you what will happen; and I'm not psychic! I've seen it happen over and over again. First of all, when you make a habit of debriefing, the critical comments you come up with in subsequent weeks will be fewer and fewer. Debriefing helps you recognize places that need reinforcing, and when you recognize them, you are both your own teacher and your own student; consequently, you avoid the pitfalls in the future. The second thing that will happen is that debriefing will become second nature. Evaluating will become something you enjoy rather than dread, because now you have experienced the benefits; and that makes you a better teacher. And, I don't think I need to tell you what that means for your kids.

TAG, YOU'RE IT!

You've been tagged. It's now your turn to go and touch others. Just like a child's game of tag, children's ministry is chaotic at times; be thankful there's always movement, there's always something happening, and there's always something changing.

In these pages, I hope you have learned how to prepare the site, lay the foundation, and frame the building that will become a vibrant and healthy children's ministry for your church.

Several years ago we had an all-church fellowship time in a room that was too small for the group. There was popcorn for everyone to enjoy, and you know where much of the popcorn ended up? On the floor. One of the ushers commented to the associate pastor, "Look at the mess on this floor!" to which our associate replied, "Raise your eyes and see all the people who have come." Children's ministry is messy and loud and crazy, but if you raise your eyes you'll see the beautiful children God has placed in your care. Go now, and make some mess, get loud, and go crazy. I hereby give you permission to have a mega-case of goose bumps, butterflies, and tingly sensations!

> *We will not hide these truths from our children*
> *we will tell the next generation*
> *about the glorious deeds of the* Lord.
> *about his power and his mighty wonders.*
> Psalm 78:4

APPENDIX

Directory of Curriculum Publishers

Awana Clubs International
1 E. Bode Rd.
Streamwood, IL 60107-6658
(630) 213-2000
www.awana.org

OneVine
Bible Alive curriculum
P.O. Box 680535
Franklin, TN 37068-0535
(615) 557-6105
www.onevine.com

Child Evangelism Fellowship, Inc.
P.O. Box 348
Warrenton, MO 63383
(636) 456-4321
www.cefpress.com

ChildrensChurchStuff.com
428 S. Seminary
Collinsville, IL 62234
(866) 774-5355
www.childrenschurchstuff.com

Children's Ministry Magazine
(for updates on material)
P.O. Box 469081
Escondido, CA 92046-9081
(877) 534-7063
www.childrensministry.com

Cokesbury
201 Eighth Ave. S.
Nashville, TN 37203
(800) 251-8591
www.cokesbury.com

David. C. Cook
4050 Lee Vance View
Colorado Springs, CO 80918
(800) 708-5550 or (719) 536-0100
www.cookministries.com

Gospel Light
1957 Eastman Ave.
Ventura, CA 93003
(800) 446-7735
www.gospellight.com

Group Publishing, Inc.
P.O. Box 481
Loveland, CO 80539
(800) 447-1070
www.group.com

High Voltage Kids Ministry
4501 Burrow Dr.
North Little Rock, AR 72116
(888) 826-4883
www.highvoltage-kids.com

Kidmo
1113 Murfreesboro Rd.,
Ste #106-145
Franklin, TN 37064
(877) 610-2935
www.kidmo.com

Kids Kount Publishing
11615 "I" Street, Ste. 3
Omaha, NE 68137
(888) 549-8687
www.kidskountpublishing.com

Kidzmatter
765 W. Gardner Dr.
Marion, IN 46952-1822
(877) 568.2437
www.kidzmatter.com

Lifeway
One LifeWay Plaza
Nashville, TN 37234
(800) 458-2772
www.lifeway.com

One Way Street Inc.
P.O. Box 5077
Englewood, CO 80155-5077
(800) 569-4537
www.onewaystreet.com

Pioneer Clubs
(800) 694-2582
www.shoppioneerclubs.org

Promiseland
Willow Creek Association
P.O. Box 3811
Barrington, IL 60011
(800) 570-9812
www.promiselandonline.com

River's Edge Curriculum
15681 79th St. NE
Elk River, MN 55330
(763) 370-3271
www.riversec.com

Standard Publishing
8805 Governor's Hill Drive, Ste. 400
Cincinnati, OH 45249
(800) 543-1353
www.standardpub.com

Warner Press
P.O. Box 2499
Anderson, IN 46018-9988
(800) 741-7721
www.warnerpress.com

Zondervan
5300 Patterson Ave. SE
Grand Rapids, MI 49530
(800) 727-3480
www.zonderkidz.com

INDEX

I

inspiration – 24, 172–179
intelligences, multiple – 65–73, 90, 103, 118, 188
intentionality – 29, 56, 78, 92

J

job descriptions – 88–92

L

leadership – 10, 13, 17, 24–35, 36, 41, 47–48, 56–58, 81, 82, 83, 88, 157, 179, 189, 190, 194

M

mailing list – 123–132, 147
mediocrity – 25
meetings – 30, 184
mentoring – 31
mission statement – 7–15, 43, 96, 100, 102, 188
momentum – 45, 49–60
motivation – 17, 32–33, 182, 187–189
multiple intelligences – 65–73, 90, 103, 118, 188

N

neuropaths – 5, 170

O

objectives – 7–15, 57, 59, 92–98, 102, 104, 105, 141
organization – 32, 117, 149, 154, 161

P

parents – 41, 156–158
passion – 21, 23, 38, 44, 88, 179
pastoral staff – 41, 45
perfection – 24, 39
policy – 111, 113, 114–115, 162
prayer – 21, 28, 35–37, 47, 62, 69, 119, 121
programming – 8, 10, 96–101
publicity – 45, 96, 98, 99, 125, 132, 136, 141–148, 192
purpose statement – 7–15, 43, 96, 100, 102, 188

R

recruiting – 45, 48, 49, 73–88, 90, 134, 180–181, 192
rejection – 26
relationships – 26, 36, 40–43, 55, 78–80, 94, 99, 112, 123, 126, 165, 173–174, 185
resources – 24, 31, 38, 57, 89, 98, 105, 106, 136, 142, 151–156, 174, 177, 186

S

safety – 106–115
senior pastor – 41, 43–48, 143, 157
servant attitude – 24
spiritual development – 72–73
spiritual growth – 35, 75, 89, 91, 96, 98, 104, 118
statement of purpose – 7–15, 43, 96, 100, 102, 188
support staff – 82

T

team development – 25, 179–189
time management – 27, 30, 85–86, 90, 187
training – 57, 77, 84, 98, 136, 179–189, 194
truth – 6, 39–40

V

vision – 16–23, 29, 33, 35, 36, 40, 41, 43, 50, 76, 78, 80, 83, 134, 135, 138, 182–183
volunteers – 17, 19, 25–27, 31, 36, 38, 57–58, 73–88, 113, 125, 137, 152, 154, 157, 177, 181–183, 185–189

W

welcoming – 22, 119, 148–151, 155
worship leader – 41, 47, 52

Y

youth pastor – 41, 132